TEENS ~ IT'S TIME TO GROW UP

Facilitator Reproducible Activities for Groups and Individuals

Ester R.A. Leutenberg

Carol Butler, MS Ed, RN, C

Illustrated by
Amy L. Brodsky, LISW-S

Duluth, Minnesota

Whole Person
101 West 2nd St., Suite 203
Duluth, MN 55802

800-247-6789

books@wholeperson.com
www.wholeperson.com

Teens – It's Time to Grow Up
Facilitator Reproducible Activities for Groups and Individuals

Copyright ©2013 by Ester R.A. Leutenberg and Carol Butler. All rights reserved. Except for short excerpts for review purposes and materials in the activities and handouts sections, no part of this book may be reproduced or transmitted in any form by any means, electronic or mechanical without permission in writing from the publisher. Activities and handouts are meant to be photocopied.

All efforts have been made to ensure accuracy of the information contained in this book as of the date published. The author(s) and the publisher expressly disclaim responsibility for any adverse effects arising from the use or application of the information contained herein.

Printed in the United States of America

10 9 8 7 6 5 4 3 2 1

Editorial Director: Carlene Sippola
Art Director: Joy Morgan Dey

Library of Congress Control Number: 2013936472
ISBN: 978-157025-302-7

Introduction

Purpose of the Book

Adolescents, like most people, crave adult privileges yet cling to childish comforts. Teens who tire of adult advice listen to peers and messages from icons of popular culture. Some teens submit blindly to authority; some respect it; others rebel. Ideally teens will be receptive to wisdom but not controlled by commands; able to discern positive from negative peer pressure and media messages; and capable of monitoring and motivating themselves.

Teens ~ It's Time to Grow Up helps teens learn, develop, mature and self-actualize with games, mock videos (skits or role plays for which teens prepare a possible video presentation), interviews, team activities, drawing, journaling, debates, discussion and other modes.
These activities guide teens in many directions:

- Grow in maturity.
- Learn from personal and others' experiences.
- Compare immature and mature ideas and actions.
- Adopt positive and assertive thoughts and behaviors.
- Apply quotations, lyrics and poems to real life.
- Make analogies between G.P.S. (global positioning devices) and individual self-righting capabilities.
- Define life lessons from favorite activities like sports and driving.
- Understand the effects of parental styles; self-parent as needed.
- Differentiate between love and infatuation, crushes and committed partnerships.
- Identify superhero and real role model traits to emulate.
- Serve as a positive influence on others.
- Determine the significance of values versus valuables.
- Acquire or enhance virtues.
- Become self-directed and determined to meet goals.
- State strengths derived from adversity (protective factors vs. risk factors).
- Recognize self as a potential late bloomer and flourish.
- Develop future dreams and ways to pursue passions.

Why this approach?
Teens may tune out adult efforts to teach and preach.
Teens tune into activities, peer involvements, opinion formations and free expressions because...
Teens take the lead.

Process trumps content as teens engage in the following:

- Introspect and interact
- Help self and others
- Brainstorm
- Problem-solve
- Confide
- Collaborate
- Uncover inborn gifts
- Fulfill potential

Aren't these the essence of adulthood?

Format of the Book

An Introduction for Participants to motivate teens for the activities (Page vi).

Seven chapters, four to nine sessions per chapter, encompass the following:

1. **RE-gress or PRO-gress?**
   Security blankets, stages, delayed gratification, to crawl or walk, whine or affirm, are pondered.
2. **Life Skills**
   Sandboxes, bikes, sports, pets, the senses, railroads, road rules and driving directions provide lessons.
3. **Parents, Partners and Role Models**
   Parent profiles, idols and ideals, relationships and red flags, leaders and followers are featured.
4. **Home, School and Work**
   Family roles, behavior behind closed doors, students, teachers, yearbook analogies, challenges and work habits are addressed.
5. **Tangible and Intangible**
   Materialism, money, monetary and behavioral costs versus benefits, values and ethics are explored.
6. **The Journey to Maturity**
   Growth through fertilizer, late bloomers, rites of passage, frozen then freed, gladiator mentality, measures of maturity, perspectives, continuums and sex sense receive focus.
7. **Life after High School**
   Education and training, career calls, love and partner traits.

Each chapter may serve as a workshop; provide one session per day for a series of days. Posters or flyers might promote the theme in advance; emphasize the interactive and collaborative nature of the sessions.

Facilitator's Table of Contents and Summary for each chapter provides a related quotation and brief session descriptions.

A reproducible handout for the participants for each session; most adapt to individual or group activities. Read each handout before session, photocopy and white out or add text for a specific population's needs; then reproduce the page and distribute. Some sessions use one handout per teen; others need to be cut on broken lines, etc.

For the Facilitator on the back of each handout tells how to use the page. It includes:

   I. Purpose: goals for teens
   II. General Comments: brief background information
   III. Possible Activities: ideas to introduce the topic, interactive and/or individual activities
   IV. Enrichment Activities: additional learning opportunities

Most sessions provide more than enough material for a **fifty-minute session**; if more time is needed facilitators may assign homework or continue topics at the next meeting.

Delicate subjects are addressed, particularly in Sex Sense; **facilitator discretion is advised**.

Facilitators are reminded to refer troubled teens for a psychiatric evaluation if they appear severely depressed, admit to thoughts about harm to self and/or others, have been or are being abused, or based on your intuition, indicate they need more help. Follow all legal reporting requirements. If threats are imminent, call 911 or your local emergency services number.

Teens need to know that keeping secrets can kill. If aware that a peer wants to harm self or others, teens need to tell a trusted adult. To break a confidence to save a life is honorable and mature.

Ideas to Facilitate Groups and Growth

Consider the Self-Fulfilling Prophesy
Participants treated like children will act like children.
Participants talked down to or talked at will turn off.
Participants will live up to expectations to think intelligently, behave unselfishly and maximize potentials.

Teens ~ It's Time to Grow Up warrants mature methods to educate and empower.

When possible …
- Ask don't tell.
- Listen to teens.
- Encourage a forum format; one person at a time speaks; teens respect divergent views.
- Promote fun through adult-type games.
- Elicit expression through role plays, pantomimes, verbal and non-verbal communication.
- Provide leadership opportunities (teens play game show host or write on the board, etc.).
- Emphasize teamwork.
- Expect movement within activities; do not expect teens to sit like statues in a lecture hall.
- Set up chairs in a circle for most sessions, but prepare to rearrange seats (for peers to collaborate, for teams to face each other, for watching skits or debates).
- Support preferences to disclose information or maintain privacy.

Remind teens to use code names for confidentiality. Example: If friend Sue loves to swim, use *SLS* for *She loves swimming*; only the writer knows the true identity.

This English 18th century proverb applies to today's teens: *Give credit where credit is due.*

Recognize, reinforce, and reward adolescent efforts to grow up.
Teens, like most people, are works in progress.

Deepest Gratitude

Our gratitude to these teen counselors for their input …

Annette Damien, MS, PPS
Beth Jennings, CTEC Counselor

And to these professionals who make us look good!

Art Director – Joy Dey
Editor and Lifelong Teacher – Eileen Regen
Editorial Director – Carlene Sippola
Illustrator – Amy L. Brodsky
Proofreader – Jay Leutenberg

Introduction for Teen Participants

> *Standing on the fringes of life offers a unique perspective.*
> *But there comes a time to see what it looks like from the dance floor.*
>
> ~ Stephen Chbosky
>
> From *The Perks of Being a Wallflower*, a novel about growing up.

Do you feel like you're on the fringes?
Do you believe you're on the brink of something big?
Do you seem torn between childish comforts and grown-up challenges?
Do you want the freedom and privileges of adulthood?

The activities in **Teens ~ It's Time to Grow Up** help you take healthy risks, to enter life's arena.

You'll have the chance to play adult-type games, perform in and/or watch mock videos, work with teammates, brainstorm, draw, journal, discuss, debate, stand up for your beliefs, share your thoughts and maintain privacy.

A few ground rules for groups and growth:

- Be honest with yourself when journaling.
- If something is inappropriate to share with others, talk with a counselor or trusted adult.
- Respect your beliefs but consider others' rights to express their views.
- One person at a time talks; do not interrupt.
- These groups are a safe place and what is revealed should not be repeated.
- Write and draw for you, yourself, not for class or publication; you decide who sees your work.
- Be a healthy risk-taker: narrate, act in a role play or pantomime; be silly in charades.
- Volunteer to be a leader, play game show host, be a scorekeeper or write peers' ideas on the board.
- If you prefer to think, watch and listen, feel free to be yourself; there's no pressure to participate.
- Ask for help from your facilitator or a trusted adult if you feel depressed or overwhelmed or need someone to listen.

When you write or share, use code names to protect confidentiality. Example: If your friend Sue loves to swim, use *SLS* for *She loves swimming*; only you know the true identity.

If you want to harm yourself or others or if a peer reveals suicidal or violent feelings, tell a trusted adult, call 911 or your local emergency services number or go to your nearest hospital emergency room. SECRETS KILL.

To break a confidence to save a life is honorable and mature.

Teens ~ *It's Time to Grow Up*

TABLE OF CONTENTS

1. RE-GRESS OR PRO-GRESS? ... 9
- You Can't Go Back ... 11
- Whom Do You Trust? ... 13
- Instant Gratification ... 15
- Then and Now ... 17
- Crawl or Walk Tall? ... 19
- Whine or Affirm? ... 21

2. LIFE SKILLS ... 23
- Sandbox Guru ... 25
- Bike Talk ... 27
- Sports Actions ... 29
- Guess Who? ... 31
- Common Sense ... 33
- Helen Keller Quotes ... 35
- Railroad Crossings ... 37
- Rules of the Road BINGO ... 39
- GPS - Global Positioning System ... 41

3. PARENTS, CARE-PROVIDERS, PARTNERS AND ROLE-MODELS ... 43
- Care-Provider Profiles ... 45
- Superheroes ... 47
- Romantic Partners ... 49
- Is it Love or Infatuation??? ... 51
- Simon and the Leader ... 53

4. HOME, SCHOOL AND WORK 55
- Role Renovations 57
- Charity Begins 59
- Yearbook 61
- Are You Ready? 63
- The Three R's 65
- My Challenges 67
- Fix Ten 69

5. TANGIBLE AND INTANGIBLE 71
- Bigger and Better 73
- Budget Breakdown 75
- Expense Exchange 77
- Alphabet Soup 79
- Your Move 81

6. THE JOURNEY TO MATURITY 83
- Dirt or Soil? 85
- Bloomer Mixer 87
- Rites and Responsibilities 89
- Freeze Tag 91
- Gladiator or Gopher? 93
- Am I There Yet? 95
- Perspectives (It's All How You Look at It) 97
- Continuums 99
- Sex Sense 101

7. LFE AFTER HIGH SCHOOL 103
- Future Feud 105
- Your Vision 107
- Do What You Love 109
- Love 111

RE-GRESS OR PRO-GRESS

The great thing in the world is not so much where we stand, as in what direction we are moving.
— OLIVER WENDELL HOLMES

You Can't Go Back .... page 11 ▶
Teens recognize possible regressive tendencies and adopt more mature ways to meet needs. Teens differentiate between security blankets and true well-being; between emotional pacifiers and real sustenance.

Whom Do You Trust? .... page 13 ▶
Through a simulated talk show or newspaper interview, teens address past and present trust issues, trustworthiness, and faith in self. Additionally, teens may portray trust via posters, mock videos and commercials, slogans, songs and poems.

INSTANT GRATIFICATION .... page 15 ▶
Teens are encouraged to value future rewards and character development over quick fixes. Realistic situations address impulsivity, aggression, peer pressure, quick money, unethical gains, etc. Teens consider diligence, self-respect, compassion and other attributes.

Then and Now .... page 17 ▶
With a Jeopardy-type game, teens apply some of Erikson's stages of development to their past, present and future. Teens give real life examples related to autonomy, initiative, industry, identity, intimacy, and other concepts.

Crawl or Walk Tall? .... page 19 ▶
Using game format, teens consider whether they crawl or walk tall through life. Passive responses to situations are provided; teens verbalize assertive alternatives. Teens are encouraged to take healthy risks and be authentic. In a team game, teens handle break-ups, loneliness, setbacks and other challenges.

Whine or Affirm? .... page 21 ▶
In a team game, teens change hopeless, helpless self-talk to empowering adult assertions. Teens see a choice: to blame the past, feel doomed, remain a victim, compare self with others, etc.; or to take inventory about self, rise above adversity, celebrate uniqueness, advocate for self, learn to cope and take other positive actions.

RE-gress or PRO-gress?

You Can't Go Back

1. **During infancy, all of your needs were probably met. How do you now try to return to an easier way?**

   Example: *Expect parents or care-providers to clean my room, cook, pay for my car and gas.*

   _____
   _____
   _____

2. **What is your current ineffective security blanket?**

   Example: *Wearing the latest trends; alcohol and drugs.*

   _____
   _____
   _____

3. **What is your current real source of security?**

   Example: *A sense of self-worth, competence and purpose.*

   _____
   _____
   _____

4. **What is your current emotional pacifier?**

   Example: *A person; unreal because no one person can provide everything; eating to forget troubles.*

   _____
   _____
   _____

5. **What is your true emotional nourishment?**

   Example: *Positive self-talk.*

   _____
   _____
   _____

TEENS – It's Time to Grow Up

You Can't Go Back

FOR THE FACILITATOR

I. **Purpose**

To recognize possible regressive tendencies and consider more effective ways to meet needs.

II. **General Comments**

Teens want to grow up yet seek some comforts of infancy.

III. **Possible Activities**
   a. If possible, show a picture of a baby thumb-sucking or ask a volunteer to draw one.
   b. Ask why some babies suck their thumbs; (to self-sooth).
   c. Ask teens in what ways they seek comfort.
   d. Distribute the *You Can't Go Back* handout and allow time for completion.
   e. Encourage teens to share their responses.

IV. **Enrichment Activities**

Encourage teens to elaborate on their responses and/or to discuss concepts below.

1. Examples of return to an easier way:
   - Whine to get what you want instead of asking politely or working to afford what you want.
   - Expect others to do your homework or projects for you.
   - Expect constant compliments, success in every endeavor, unconditional acceptance.

2. Examples of current ineffective security blankets:
   - Food.
   - Popularity at all costs.
   - Attractiveness, latest fashion clothing and shoes, cars.
   - Superficial friends.
   - Excessive social networking.

3. Examples of current real sources of security:
   - Feelings of self-worth, competence, purpose.
   - Supportive family, true friends.
   - Coping skills to deal with stress and disappointment.

4. Examples of current emotional pacifiers:
   - Electronics, social networks, designer clothes, status symbols, etc., unreal because they are external and temporary.
   - Attention or acceptance for going along with the crowd (acting against your beliefs).

5. Examples of true emotional nourishment:
   - Faith; spiritual strengths.
   - Appreciation of nature, art, music, literature.
   - Participation in nature, (gardening, etc.); creative endeavors.
   - Satisfaction in being your best self.
   - To work for a cause greater than you – charitable deeds, social, political, environmental activism.

RE-gress or PRO-gress?

 Whom Do You Trust?

As an infant you had no choice of care providers. Depending on whether they fed, clothed, and comforted you when you cried, you learned to trust or distrust. You now can choose people you think are trustworthy.

As a child, in what ways did you learn to trust or distrust?

_____
_____
_____
_____

How did your experiences influence your current expectations of people and relationships?

_____
_____
_____
_____

List at least three qualities that make someone trustworthy.

_____
_____
_____
_____

Share circumstances where you might not trust yourself.

_____
_____
_____
_____

In what ways do you absolutely trust yourself?

_____
_____
_____
_____

TEENS – It's Time to Grow Up

Whom Do You Trust?

FOR THE FACILITATOR

I. Purpose
To consider past and present issues regarding trust.

II. General Comments
Teens may ask and answer questions in an interview format or write responses privately.

III. Possible Activities
a. Ask teens to describe their favorite talk shows.
b. Explain they will be answering questions privately or in an interview format.
c. These are very delicate questions and if too revealing for a talk show or newspaper article format, the page can be used as a journaling activity.
d. Remind teens when journaling or sharing aloud to use name codes.

Journaling Format
- Distribute the *Whom Do You Trust?* handout and allow time for completion.
- Allow teens to share their responses within their comfort levels and as appropriate for a group setting. (Remind them to use name codes).

Talk Show Format
- Teens take turns sitting in pairs at the front of the room; one reads the questions and the other answers; then the guest who responded becomes the interviewer.
- Only the first host reads aloud the statement at the top; subsequent interviewers read only the questions.
- Peers in the audience may ask questions or provide feedback.

Newspaper Article Format
- Teens sit in pairs and take turns reading the questions and writing the partner's responses.
- They may re-convene and share their articles aloud with the group.

IV. Enrichment Activities
a. Encourage teens to brainstorm trustworthy traits; a volunteer lists their ideas on the board. Possibilities include a person who …
  - Carries out a responsibility.
  - Keeps a promise.
  - Keeps a secret (unless it involves harm to self, others, abuse, suicidal thoughts, etc.).
  - Demonstrates honesty, loyalty, reliability.
  - Acts in private the way he/she would with the world watching.

b. Encourage teens to address trust issues through activities:
  - Making posters.
  - Composing slogans, poems or song lyrics.
  - Performing mock videos or commercials.
  - Trust walk – blindfold and walk with a sighted partner over a simple, safe obstacle course.

RE-gress or PRO-gress?

INSTANT GRATIFICATION

Infants want instant gratification like hugs and bottles. Young children want what they want when they want it and scream if they don't get it. Older children can delay gratification by working all week for an allowance.

To delay gratification – by valuing future rewards and character development over quick fixes – shows maturity.

For each example below, write "I" for instant gratification or "D" for delayed gratification.

1. _____ Curse or punch in anger to let off steam.
2. _____ Go along with the crowd to be accepted.
3. _____ Decide to take time out when angry.
4. _____ Think hard about compromise instead of having your own way.
5. _____ Reach for food, a drug or a drink when stressed.
6. _____ Go to a party the night before final exams.
7. _____ Lie to cover a mistake.
8. _____ Learn coping skills.
9. _____ Study tonight; go out with friends after exams.
10. _____ Say yes when you want to say no to satisfy a partner.
11. _____ Drive fast for the thrill of it.
12. _____ Enter training for an occupation that interests you.
13. _____ Cheat to pass a test.
14. _____ Take what you want.
15. _____ Be a bully to show strength.
16. _____ Work, save and wait for what you want.
17. _____ Gossip in texts and e-mails to be part of the crowd.
18. _____ Spend too much money to look good on a date.
19. _____ Think before you act.
20. _____ Break-up at the first argument.
21. _____ Agree to disagree with another.

Describe your current or recent instant gratification versus delayed gratification situation.

_____

_____

_____

_____

TEENS – It's Time to Grow Up

INSTANT GRATIFICATION

FOR THE FACILITATOR

I. **Purpose**
   To recognize that delaying gratification or taking the harder route for a better outcome is beneficial.

II. **General Comments**
   Teens tend to live in the moment, but looking at risks and long-term rewards signifies maturity.

III. **Possible Activities**
   a. Ask a volunteer to display a coin or paper currency.
   b. Ask teens for a show of hands regarding this choice: Would you like to receive the observed currency amount today, or double the value tomorrow?
   c. Discuss that babies and children want immediate gratification; the ability to delay for a greater reward signifies maturity.
   d. Distribute the *Instant Gratification* handout and allow time for completion.
   e. Review responses and encourage teens to share their current instant versus delayed gratification situations and receive peer feedback.

IV. **Enrichment Activities**
   a. See answer key below, "I" or "D".
   b. Elicit concepts related to the handout; possibilities correspond to the item numbers:
      1. I – Aggression might feel good momentarily but destroys relationships; walk away from a fight.
      2. I – Acceptance may result in shame and embarrassment and losing one's self.
      3. D – To take a break to cool down allows time to plan appropriate words and actions.
      4. D – Give and take or meeting half-way are win-win strategies.
      5. I – Quick fixes may result in overweight or addiction; problems remain despite temporary escapes.
      6. I – Fun tonight might not be worth a failing grade tomorrow.
      7. I – To lie might seem an easier way out; guilt and fear of being found out may be worse.
      8. D – Coping skills take time and effort but help difficult situations and emotions.
      9. D – Stick to the task that must be done first and probably earn better grades.
      10. I – To please a partner by going against your beliefs destroys self-determination and esteem.
      11. I – Momentary pleasure may result in disability, harming or killing others or self.
      12. D – Self-discipline from completing training results in confidence as well as financial benefits.
      13. I – Gain a grade, lose integrity and live in fear of being found out.
      14. I – Items taken illegally or unethically rarely bring lasting pleasure; earning enhances the earner.
      15. I – Show strength through compassion, help others and be a leader by example.
      16. D – Perseverance and patience are gained, whether or not you get what you originally wanted.
      17. I – To know but not tell shows maturity and empathy.
      18. I – Appearance or amounts spent on entertainment matter less than showing interest in your partner.
      19. D – Consider options and their consequences to make better decisions.
      20. I – To know when to work on relationships and when to leave toxic ones shows discernment.
      21. D – Some issues allow for differing viewpoints.

RE-gress or PRO-gress? ▶

Then and Now

Autonomy
1. Describe a time you said *no* just to be defiant
2. Describe a time you respectfully said *no* for a good reason.
3. In childhood, how did your care providers respond when you tried to do things for yourself?
4. Share examples of your care providers applauding your efforts to be self-sufficient.
5. How does your family react when you disagree?
6. Are you too dependent or too independent? How?

Initiative
1. How did your care providers handle your risk-taking, like learning to ride a bike or cross streets?
2. To what extent were you allowed to make decisions about what to wear or foods to eat?
3. Give examples regarding your tendencies now to lead or follow.
4. Give examples showing whether you are a self-starter or need to be pushed to perform tasks.
5. What are you doing to improve your life?
6. How might a person overcome guilt?

Industry
1. Share how you were encouraged or put down when you first learned to read and write.
2. What were your early interests and how do you ignore or incorporate them into your life?
3. Give examples regarding your tendency to stick to a task or to give up easily.
4. Share how you currently tend to procrastinate or persevere in facing challenges.
5. Does hard work pay off for you? Why or why not?
6. How might a person overcome feelings of inferiority?

Identity
1. What three words best describe your personality and why?
2. Name at least three abilities you have or hope to develop.
3. Name three careers you might pursue and tell why they appeal to you.
4. What three things matter most to you and why?
5. Describe your basic beliefs about people, a social or political issue, or your faith.
6. In three words who are you?

Intimacy
1. What did you learn from your first romantic relationship?
2. Describe how you have handled rejection in the past.
3. How do you define emotional intimacy and a reciprocal relationship?
4. Give examples of how you either try to blend in or how you stand out among peers.
5. Describe barriers, healthy boundaries and lack of boundaries in relationships.
6. If you feel alone what can you do?

TEENS – It's Time to Grow Up

Then and Now

FOR THE FACILITATOR

I. Purpose

To apply some of Erikson's stages of development to past and present experiences.

II. General Comments

Teens consider autonomy, initiative, industry, identity and intimacy issues. (Trust is addressed in the session *Whom Do You Trust?, pages 13 and 14*).

III. Possible Activities

a. Before session photocopy the Then and Now handout and cut on the broken lines.

b. List the categories on the board: *Autonomy, Initiative, Industry, Identity, Intimacy*.

Game Format

- Ask five volunteers who are comfortable reading aloud to sit in the front of the room.
- Each selects a category and receives the corresponding cut-out list of questions.
- Teens take turns selecting a topic; volunteer with that topic reads the question, and the peer responds.
- There are no right or wrong answers; teens share what is true for them.

Team Format

- Teens select categories and sit close to teammates who chose the same topic.
- Teams receive a photocopy of the corresponding questions.
- A team leader asks the questions; teammates take turns answering.
- Facilitator circulates among the teams, listening and reinforcing insightful responses.

Individual Format

- Individual teens select categories and receive the corresponding list of questions, (or the entire uncut handout).
- They respond in writing on a separate paper and /or share answers aloud.

c. For all formats, conclude by encouraging teens to share which category is most applicable to them now and how they are mastering its challenges.

IV. Enrichment Activities

a. Write on the board *Make your life count*.

b. Ask teens to discuss ways they can make their current and future lives count, how they might improve society, be productive and/or creative.

c. Ask teens to discuss ways they can act now to be proud about later, how they might accomplish goals, make ethical decisions and limit potential regrets.

RE-gress or PRO-gress?

Crawl or Walk Tall?

#		#		#		#		#	
1	You neither ask nor answer questions in class.	2	Your friends bully and gossip; you keep quiet.	3	You wait for others to make the first move toward friendship.	4	You love writing but won't join the writing club.	5	You want to date someone but are afraid to ask.
6	People often borrow from you; you won't say no.	7	You are being abused and heed the warnings to never tell.	8	You dented the car and wait worriedly until your parents see it.	9	Someone wronged you; you tell everyone or no one.	10	You hurt someone but don't apologize; you think they deserved it!
11	You received a low grade; you blame the teacher.	12	You resent someone who does better in a sport.	13	You have no friends; you go straight home after school.	14	Your boy/girlfriend broke up with you; you decide you are worthless.	15	A friend betrayed you; you decide to trust no one.
16	You don't look like a movie star or jock; you feel ugly.	17	Peers urge you to cheat or steal; you agree to avoid rejection.	18	An adult says you'll never amount to anything; you believe the person.	19	A partner wants you to do his/her assignment; you agree.	20	A struggling student needs a study partner but you are too busy.
21	You are wrongly accused; you suffer in silence.	22	You turn down a job you might like because you fear failure.	23	You love art; you won't enter a poster contest because you might not win.	24	You put off a project because you can't do it perfectly.	25	Your boy/girlfriend degrades you but you stay with the person.
26	You believe it when you are told your goals are impossible.	27	You lose a contest or game; you decide to never try again.	28	You hide part of your identity fearing disapproval will devastate you.	29	You will not admit a problem or ask for help.	30	You want more money; you expect to get it from your family.

TEENS – It's Time to Grow Up

Crawl or Walk Tall?

FOR THE FACILITATOR

I. Purpose
To recognize passive behavior as immature *crawling*; to decide assertiveness, *walking*, is mature.

II. General Comments
Teens can be put down by adults, peers or their own negative thinking. They consider how to *stand up* to inhibiting influences.

III. Possible Activities
a. Before session photocopy the *Crawl or Walk Tall?* handout and cut on the broken lines.
b. Place cut-outs in a container.
c. Ask what it would be like to *crawl* through life, (other people always above; get stepped on).
d. Ask what is accomplished by *walking*, (put people on equal levels; ability to choose to stay or leave.).
e. Teens take turns reading a cut-out aloud and substituting an assertive, *walking* behavior for the childish *crawling* passivity; peers can help or add ideas. Possible responses include:
   1. Take risks, ask and answer, this contributes to learning and makes class more fun.
   2. Speak up against bullying, defend the person being bullied, or tell staff anonymously.
   3. Ask a question, show interest in others; comment about or compliment something about a peer.
   4. Join the club, or ask to work on the school paper; do not feed your fear of not doing well enough.
   5. Ask; if refused, find someone who is like-minded in a class or extracurricular activity.
   6. Say *no* when necessary, true friends will understand; others won't.
   7. Stand up for your life, health and sanity; tell a trusted teacher or counselor.
   8. Tell your parents; accept the blame and offer to pay for repairs.
   9. Tell the person how you feel and how you want to be treated.
   10. Apologize; do the right thing regardless of what you think they deserve.
   11. Take responsibility; accept that you are not great at everything; ask for extra instruction.
   12. Ask how to improve; watch to pick up pointers; play for the fun of it – you need not be the best.
   13. Go to an after school club, activity, sport, job or volunteer site to meet people.
   14. Decide the relationship was not the lasting type; you have much to offer the right person.
   15. Trust people in small ways at first until they prove trustworthy.
   16. Define and play up your unique physical qualities; develop attractive internal traits and personality.
   17. Say *no*; find friends whose values are compatible with yours.
   18. Adults can be wrong; your own beliefs and perseverance determine who you are and who you will become.
   19. Explain you cannot do it for them; offer suggestions or resources to help them.
   20. Try to find a limited amount of time or share tips for efficient and effective study habits or tutors.
   21. Defend yourself calmly to your accuser; go to an authority if necessary.
   22. Take the job; not trying is the biggest failure; if you make mistakes, learn from them.
   23. Enter the contest; winning is over-rated; put yourself and your work out there.
   24. Perfection is rarely achieved; your best is usually good enough.
   25. Ask them to stop; if they don't, upgrade yourself by ending the relationship.
   26. Let no one discourage you; seek people who encourage and mentor you.
   27. You will learn from the experience; decide to try again.
   28. Reveal the real you to people you love; hope for acceptance; know you'll survive criticism.
   29. Acknowledge the problem; accept help; later you'll be able to help others in similar situations.
   30. Ask family what you can do to earn money. Begin to budget.

IV. Enrichment Activities
Encourage teens to share current challenges; peers suggest ways to *walk tall* not *crawl*.

RE-gress or PRO-gress?

Whine or Affirm?

Team A
Read aloud the whines below; the other team will substitute affirmations.

1. Poor me. My parents don't have much money.
2. I'm ruined for life because I was abused.
3. It's everyone else's fault that I'm miserable.
4. I'll always be this way.
5. Nobody appreciates me.
6. Everyone else gets all the breaks.
7. I can't change.
8. I'm doomed because of my dysfunctional family.
9. I drink or use drugs to escape my terrible life.
10. Nothing good comes out of my neighborhood.

Brainstorm with your team and list your own whines; the other team will substitute affirmations.

1. _____
2. _____
3. _____
4. _____
5. _____

Team B
Read aloud the whines below; the other team will substitute affirmations.

1. I'm unlucky.
2. I'm a victim.
3. Nobody ever helps me.
4. I have a mental block when it comes to math.
5. I can't do anything right.
6. Everyone is against me.
7. I'm not college material.
8. My parents' divorce messed me up.
9. I'm spoiled because my parents gave in too often and gave me too much.
10. I can't measure up to my sibling.

Brainstorm with your team and list your own whines; the other team will substitute affirmations.

1. _____
2. _____
3. _____
4. _____
5. _____

TEENS – It's Time to Grow Up

Whine or Affirm?

FOR THE FACILITATOR

I. **Purpose**

To change hopeless, helpless, immature self-talk to empowering assertions.

II. **General Comments**

Taking responsibility for self and deciding on positivity are productive and mature actions.

III. **Possible Activities**

a. Before session, photocopy the *Whine or Affirm?* handout and cut on the broken line.
b. Fill a glass half way. Ask for a show of hands, *"Who sees the glass half full?"* Then, ask *"Who sees the glass half empty?"* Explain, *"This is the difference between optimists and pessimists."*
c. Ask teens what age group tends to whine, (young children).
d. Ask if older people can become whiners, (yes, chronic complainers).
e. Divide the teens into two teams and arrange two rows of chairs facing each other.
f. Each team receives a list of ten whines; teens take turns reading a whine to the person facing them (opponent) who substitutes an affirmation; then they reverse roles.
Example: The first teen in Team A reads Number 1 from their list to the first teen in Team B who states a corresponding affirmation; then they reverse roles. Both pass their papers to the teammates next to them; the second teen in each team reads Number 2 to the opponent, who substitutes an affirmation. This continues until all have a turn.
g. Teens may ask teammates for help if they have difficulty; no one is set up to be embarrassed.

Possible affirmations for the Team A list:

1. I can change my financial situation; I may be rich by having a great family or other blessings.
2. I can become stronger; I can help others who experience abuse.
3. I take responsibility for my reactions and emotions; I can end the misery by becoming more positive.
4. I can learn coping skills; I can ask for counseling.
5. I appreciate me; I'm grateful for my abilities. I'll be sure to thank others for kindness or help.
6. I can make or break myself by how I think and what I do.
7. I can change; moving out of my comfort zone will be challenging but rewarding.
8. I recognize and will rise above their dysfunction; I'll seek professional help if needed.
9. I can choose mental health and sobriety to survive and thrive; I can help others in recovery.
10. Many successful people had humble beginnings; **my** *mental neighborhood* matters most.

Possible Affirmations for the Team B list:

1. My luck will improve if I take advantage of opportunities and do my best.
2. I'm a survivor, a victor, a stronger person who faced and learned from adversity.
3. I can help myself and I'll help others which will make me feel good.
4. I'll ask for tutoring, I'll do extra homework and I'll re-take a class if needed.
5. I can do many things right; I can work on my weaknesses and I can capitalize on my strengths.
6. I'll try to find out why and I'll correct my offensive behaviors.
7. I'm uniquely gifted for my passion; I'll meet the challenge of college or get other training.
8. I'm emerging stronger from a difficult situation; I understand more about relationships.
9. I can accept not getting my own way; I appreciate what I have but am willing to work for things.
10. I'll celebrate who I am and who my sibling is; we each have different but special things about us.

IV. **Enrichment Activities**

a. Teammates huddle out of the other team's hearing range.
b. Teams develop and write the additional five whines, re-convene and read aloud to each other as in the original activity; opponents state corresponding affirmations.

LIFE SKILLS 2

*Look closely at the present you are constructing:
It should look like the future you are dreaming.*
— ALICE WALKER

Sandbox Guru .... page 25 ▶

Teens apply sandbox lessons to life: jump in with both feet (be enthused), build sand castles (dream big but start from the bottom up), get dirty (learn from trials and errors) and other analogies.

Bike Talk .... page 27 ▶

Teens relate bicycle quotations and terminology to maturity. Examples: tires – patch problems before they get big and inflate with the right amount of self-confidence; kickstand – stand independently or pause to reconsider and recharge; pedals – propel with positive visualization, preparation and push harder as warranted; road rash – learn from the fall and heal emotional abrasions.

SPORTS ACTIONS .... page 29 ▶

Teens portray sports through charades then apply sports metaphors to growth and life: how to step up to the plate, run one's own race, be one's own cheerleader, define internal and external lift tickets, learn from Monday morning quarterbacking, skate from thin ice to solid footing, and other comparisons.

Guess Who? .... page 31 ▶

Teens draw or describe their favorite pets anonymously; peers match pets with their owners then apply lessons learned from pets to life. Unconditional love, non-verbal communication, mutual respect, and that messes can be cleaned up are among the lessons.

Common Sense .... page 33 ▶

In a Sense Fair format or as individuals or teams, teens identify how they have closed their eyes and ears and what they have failed to feel or touch; teens decide what they need to see, hear, experience and reach out to. Balance, pressure and motion are also addressed.

Helen Keller Quotes .... page 35 ▶

Teens connect with her wisdom, who rose above impediments in sight, speech and hearing. Teens tell how they will Look the world straight in the eye; teens personalize other phrases.

(Continued on the next page)

LIFE SKILLS *(Continued)*

Railroad Crossings .... page 37 ▶
Through a railroad crossing illustration teens think before they act, consider risks and rewards, share bells and whistles warnings, and listen to the still, small voice from their heads, hearts and from trusted advisors.

Rules of the Road BINGO .... page 39 ▶
Teens apply driving concepts to life by completing sentence starters: I apply my brakes when…; A pothole I can avoid is…; I don't dwell on my rear-view mirror because…; I've parked too long in…; I tailgate a person by … and others.

GPS–GLOBAL POSITIONING SYSTEMS ..... page 41 ▶
Teens compare driving to reaching a goal; they identify their destination, voice prompting directions, what to avoid, how they could veer off track, and their automatic re-routing plan if a wrong turn is made. Teens compare themselves to boats that right themselves when capsized, and to airplanes via positive and negative auto-pilot actions.

Sandbox Guru

As a young adult, can you relate to everything you learned in a sand box?

TEENS – It's Time to Grow Up

Sandbox Guru

FOR THE FACILITATOR

I. Purpose
   To apply sandbox lessons to life.

II. General Comments
   Teens learn through a picture that may mean more than words.

III. Possible Activities
   a. If possible present an actual sand pail and shovel.
   b. Distribute the *Sandbox Guru* handout and ask a volunteer to read the introduction aloud.

   Whole Group Discussion Format
   Ask teens to recall some childish lessons and their adult counterparts. If necessary, provide the bulleted prompts; possible teen interpretations are parenthesized.

   - Remove shoes before getting in (jump into your endeavor with both feet, enthused).
   - Use the right toys (use tools or coping skills appropriate to the situation).
   - Share your toys (help others through your time, knowledge, compassion).
   - Don't throw sand (don't hurl insults or send damaging electronic messages).
   - Get the sand out of your own eyes first (make changes in self rather than focusing on others).
   - Build sand castles (have big dreams, plan and plot their development, start from the bottom up).
   - Don't trample on others' castles (never discourage peers' dreams or put down accomplishments).
   - Make tracks with your truck (forge new ways ahead to go where you've never been).
   - Build hills and valleys, drive over the dunes, (expect ups and downs in life, surmount obstacles).
   - You might get dirty (learn from trials and errors, people rarely emerge unscathed from challenges).
   - Dust yourself off (shake off the messes or mistakes, results of risks; focus on lessons learned).
   - Child's play is their work (learn by doing, do what you love).
   - Watch and listen (learn from others, versus from *hard* knocks, when possible).
   - Have fun (enjoy the process of life and see new experiences as exciting challenges).

   Team Format
   - Teens receive the page divide into teams, and brainstorm their ideas; a writer lists them.
   - Teens re-convene and share their lists of lessons learned.

   Individual Format
   Distribute the page; teens write responses, then share insights aloud.

IV. Enrichment Activities
   Ask teens to consider other analogies such as *A Day at the Beach*.
   Possible concepts:

   - Stay near the lifeguard (allow a parent or trusted advisor to monitor you).
   - Use the buddy system (pick friends who help you stay safe; warn friends of danger).
   - Get your feet wet (test the waters – new experiences – with optimism and judgment).
   - Ride the waves (roll with or rise above circumstances beyond your control).
   - Keep your head above water (know your limits and do not take on too much).
   - Avoid undertows (steer clear of people, places, thoughts, habits that drag you down).
   - Observe red flag warnings (listen to wise advice about alcohol, drugs, dishonesty, etc.).
   - Know when to tread water (stay in place long enough to make an educated decision).
   - Know CPR (ask for help, resuscitate yourself if you start to decline, help others).

Life Skills

Bike Talk

> The bicycle is a curious vehicle.
> It's passenger is it's engine.
> ~John Howard

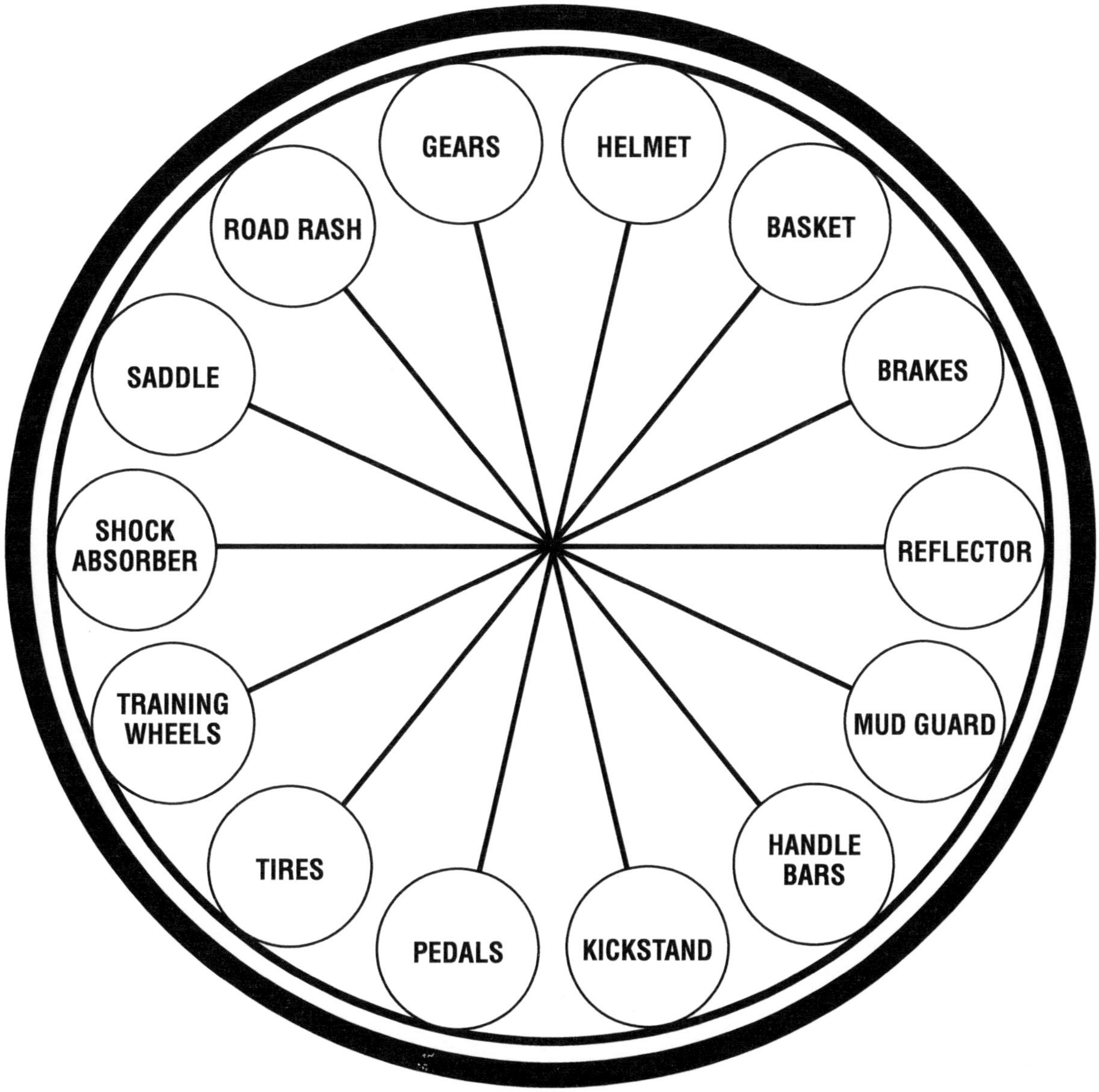

- GEARS
- HELMET
- ROAD RASH
- BASKET
- SADDLE
- BRAKES
- SHOCK ABSORBER
- REFLECTOR
- TRAINING WHEELS
- MUD GUARD
- TIRES
- HANDLE BARS
- PEDALS
- KICKSTAND

> Life is like riding a bicycle—
> in order to keep your balance, you must keep moving.
> ~Albert Einstein

TEENS – It's Time to Grow Up

Bike Talk

FOR THE FACILITATOR

I. **Purpose**
   To compare bike riding to life.

II. **General Comments**
   Teens relate quotations and terminology to mental maturity.

III. **Possible Activities**
   a. Encourage teens to share their first bicycle riding experiences and describe who taught them to ride.
   b. Distribute the *Bike Talk* handout; ask a teen to read aloud the John Howard quotation.
   c. Ask teens how they might be passenger, engine, and driver (coast along wherever life takes them; energize themselves like an engine; control their speed and direction like a driver, etc.).
   d. Ask teens to define the center of the circle, *The Zone* (losing yourself entirely in what you are doing).
   e. Ask teens to share times in sports or life they have experienced a natural high.
   f. Teens twirl a pencil on their handouts and apply the term to which it points to their lives; alternately teens may choose terms to interpret, or write responses to all, then share aloud.
      - Helmet: protect your brain; block damaging thoughts or demoralizing messages.
      - Basket: be careful what cargo you carry; avoid resentment, victimization, toxic people.
      - Brakes: know when and how to stop a detrimental habit, thought, relationship.
      - Reflector: let your light shine (talents, knowledge, compassion).
      - Mudguard: use coping skills in messy situations or when negativity is thrown at you.
      - Handlebars: steer toward your goal; watch where you focus (you'll turn in that direction).
      - Kickstand: stand independently for what you believe in; be careful where you park.
      - Pedals: propel yourself with positive visualization, preparation; push harder as needed.
      - Training wheels: obtain help but recognize when you're ready to ride on your own.
      - Tires: patch problems before they get big; *inflate* with the right amount of self-confidence.
      - Shock absorber: use inner strength and external support systems when you hit bumps.
      - Saddle: be in the environment and frame of mind to go forward and face challenges.
      - Road rash: if you suffer emotional abrasions, learn from the fall, use first aid (hope, faith).
      - Gears: adjust expectations as needed and be willing to delay gratification.
   g. Encourage a discussion of the Albert Einstein quotation.
   h. Ask teens to brainstorm ways to keep moving toward personal growth, academic achievement, better relationships, mental and physical health, skill development and other goals.

IV. **Enrichment Activities**
   a. Ask teens in what situations they need to change direction (alcohol, drugs, negative people, certain places and behaviors).
   b. Ask teens when it is advisable to stop moving, *put down the kickstand* and pause (when they need direction from trusted people, to rest and recharge and when they need time to consider options).

Life Skills

SPORTS ACTIONS

1 BASEBALL	2 RUNNING	3 BOXING	4 FISHING
5 FOOTBALL	6 HOCKEY	7 CANOEING	8 HUNTING
9 SAILING	10 ICE SKATING	11 SWIMMING	12 BASKETBALL
13 TENNIS	14 WHISTLE	15 BILLIARDS	16 TEAM
17 SKATEBOARDING	18 DIVING	19 CHEERLEADING	20 SKIING

TEENS – It's Time to Grow Up

SPORTS ACTIONS

FOR THE FACILITATOR

I. **Purpose**

Teens apply sports metaphors to growth and life.

II. **General Comments**

Many teens like and can relate to sports, however teens who do not can still relate to these questions; teens play charades, then make mature analogies.

III. **Possible Activities**
   a. Before session photocopy the *Sports Actions* handout and cut on the dotted lines.
   b. Place cut-outs in a container; if possible use a sports glove, cap or other prop.
   c. Teens take turns selecting a cut-out word and portraying it through body language, (charades).
   d. Peers guess the sport, then participants answer related questions below in "g".
   e. The next volunteer selects a cut-out and portrays a sport; peers guess then answer questions, etc.
   f. Ask the following sports related questions to the group.
   g. Teens need to be specific and action-oriented in their responses.
      1. Baseball: How will you *step up to the plate* and do something you want to do or need to do?
      2. Running: How do you plan to *run your own race and go the distance*?
      3. Boxing: Who is *in your corner* and what are they advising you to do?
      4. Fishing: In what situation do you need to *fish or cut bait*, (stick with it or exit)?
      5. Football: What have you learned from *Monday morning quarterbacking* about your actions?
      6. Hockey: What *penalty have you experienced* and how will you avoid repeating the offense?
      7. Canoeing: In what situation are you ready to or do you need to *put your oars in the water*?
      8. Hunting: When did you bark up the wrong tree and what is your *current hunting ground*?
      9. Sailing: How are you learning the ropes and letting no one take the *wind out of your sails*?
      10. Ice skating: When were you skating on thin ice and how are you now on *solid footing*?
      11. Swimming: In what situation do you need to *float instead of going against the current*?
      12. Basketball: How can you gain a *home court advantage* about a challenge you face?
      13. Tennis: What *ball is now in your court* and how do you intend to hit it?
      14. Whistle: About what did you (or would you) *blow the whistle* and why?
      15. Billiards: In what way are you *behind the eight ball* but planning to give it your best shot?
      16. Team: What qualities do want in your teammates and *what kind of team player* are you?
      17. Skateboarding: If you have been hurt, how will you heal and *get back on the skateboard*?
      18. Diving: Into what waters would you *like to plunge* and overcome fear of a nosedive?
      19. Cheerleading: In what way can you be your own cheerleader and *how high can you jump*?
      20. Skiing: Define your *internal and external lift tickets* and how you'll get to the top of the hill.

IV. **Enrichment Activities**
   a. Ask teens to portray other sports and to brainstorm related lessons, metaphors and idioms Possibilities include:
      - Fishing: open a can of worms, hit a snag, hit bottom, swallow it hook, line and sinker, be hooked on something, be on the hook, get off the hook.
      - Boating: bail out, make waves, go overboard, ride out the storm.
      - Most sports: play ball, make a game plan, keep your eye on the ball, keep it rolling.
   b. Encourage a discussion about the baseball term 'being in left field.' Ask teens to share times an unconventional position was not productive and conversely how an unusual idea or goal might benefit them.

Life Skills

Guess Who?

Draw or describe your favorite past or present pet, or an animal you hope to have some day.

Pets meet emotional needs for…
___
___
___

Pets help owners develop these qualities…
___
___
___

Guess Who?
FOR THE FACILITATOR

I. Purpose
To apply lessons learned from pets to life.

II. General Comments
Teens link pet pictures or descriptions with their peer owners, then consider emotional benefits and values of pet ownership.

III. Possible Activities
a. Explain that teens will draw or describe their favorite pets anonymously, then peers guess their owners.
b. Distribute the *Guess Who?* handout; tell teens that artistic ability, spelling and grammar do not matter.
c. Teens do not write their names on the handout; allow time for completion.
d. Teens fold their papers and place them in a container; a volunteer shuffles them to ensure random order.
e. If any teen does not want to enter a picture into the game, it is ok; respect each other's privacy.
f. Teens take turns going to the front of the room, picking up a pet picture, and guessing its owner.
g. Teens then show the picture or read the description aloud and the owner claims the page.
h. After teens finish the guessing game, encourage them to share their sentence completions.

IV. Enrichment Activities
a. Encourage teens to discuss emotional benefits:
   - **Unconditional, non-judgmental love:** to be able to tell secrets and share feelings.
   - **Experience the life-cycle:** rejoice at birth; develop empathy when illness or injury occurs; learn to deal with grief and loss.
   - **Read non-verbal cues:** recognize that pets feel angry, sad, jealous, fearful at times too.
b. Encourage teens to discuss the qualities developed in pet owners that prepare them for life:
   - **Responsibility for living creatures** dependent upon them for food, water, attention.
   - **Respect for animal and human differences** (likes, dislikes, needs).
   - **Mastery to ensure safety and teach simple tricks** (transferrable to a sense of competence and confidence in other relationships and endeavors).
   - **Resourcefulness to entertain the pet and make toys** (transferrable to creativity in life).
   - **Realization that animals like people need limits plus freedom** depending on their maturity level.
   - **Knowledge that relationships are based on mutual respect** (meeting each other's needs, spending quality time together and having fun).
   - **Understanding** that even in the closest relationships **animals and people need opportunities** to explore other interests.
   - **Recognition that messes** (mistakes, conflicts) can be cleaned up.

Life Skills

Common Sense

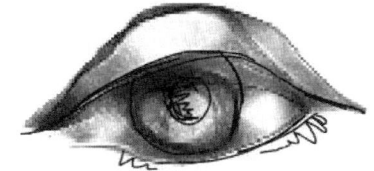

I did not want to see …   I now see …

I did not want to hear…   I now listen to…

I did not let myself feel…   I now feel…

I did not touch…   I now reach out to…

TEENS – It's Time to Grow Up

Common Sense

FOR THE FACILITATOR

I. **Purpose**
   To figuratively develop the inborn senses.

II. **General Comments**
   Teens may close their eyes and ears to things they do not want to take in; even youth may have hardened hearts; teens may need to reach out and touch positive possibilities.

III. **Possible Activities**
   a. Before session photocopy and cut the *Common Sense* handout on the broken lines.
   b. Tell teens that as babies their senses were not fully developed but as teens they have full capability.
   c. Ask for examples of looking at something but not really seeing, listening but not hearing (not noticing the details of something seen, not paying attention to what is said).

   Sense Stations or Sense Fair Format
   - Tape each illustration to a large piece of paper and tape one paper onto each of four walls; or tape each onto a smaller paper and attach each to a clipboard; a volunteer hosts each station, and encourages peers to write or lists their ideas for them.
   - Teens move around the room; each adds at least one item under each sentence starter.
   - Then volunteers take the pages off the walls or clipboards and read the lists aloud.

   Team or Individual Format
   - Either cut the handout on broken lines or leave it uncut.
   - Distribute a body part cut out or the entire page to teams or individuals.
   - Teams elect a writer who lists their ideas; individuals complete their own page.
   - Writers or individuals share their lists. Possibilities:

I did not want to see… The truth about a dating partner. A weakness within myself. A step I need to take.	I now see… Signs of an abusive partner. A trait I need to change. A possibility to improve myself.
I did not want to hear… Advice from a parent. Constructive criticism. That I had a problem.	I now listen to… The voice of reason and experience. Helpful suggestions. People who overcame my problem.
I did not let myself feel… Pain because it would hurt. Hope because I might deflate. Affection because it might not be returned.	I now feel… Discomfort as a part of life. Optimism that I'll handle whatever comes. Affection as long as the relationship is healthy.
I did not touch… People who were different or who might reject me. Obstacles for fear of failure. Aspirations that might not be achieved.	I now reach out to… Those needing compassion; prospective friends. Challenges with positive self-talk. My heart, my dreams, my potential, my possibilities.

IV. **Enrichment Activities**
   Ask teens to discuss their inborn abilities or sensations of balance, pressure and motion.
   - Balance: between work and play, social life and solitude, helping others and meeting personal needs.
   - Pressures: positive and negative peer pressure, academic or athletic competition, parental pressure to be something they are not, or to be all they can be, social expectations, etc.
   - Motion: How are they on a fast track to destruction or success. How can they move steadily toward goals and avoid stagnation?

Life Skills

Helen Keller Quotes

Alone we can do so little; together we can do so much.
With whom might you join efforts and what will you accomplish?

Everything has its wonders, even darkness and silence, and I learn whatever state I may be in, therein to be content.
How can you be content in your current condition(s)?

While they were saying amongst themselves it cannot be done, it was done.
What do you believe can be done that others don't? How?

Self-pity is our worst enemy and if we yield to it, we can never do anything wise in the world.
Without self-pity, what wise actions will you take?

It's a terrible thing to see and have no vision.
State your positive prediction about righting a wrong (in your life or society).

Keep your face to the sunshine and you cannot see a shadow.
What optimistic idea will you focus on?

The world is full of suffering. It is also full of overcoming.
What are you overcoming?

Never bend your head. Always hold it high. Look the world straight in the eye.
Who or what will you look straight in the eye and how?

Life is either a great adventure or nothing.
What do you want to be more adventurous about? How?

When we do the best we can, we never know what miracle is wrought in our life or the life of another.
In what endeavor are you doing your best and hoping for a miracle?

One can never consent to creep when one feels an impulse to soar.
What urges you to reach sky high?

We would never learn to be brave and patient if there were only joy in the world.
What circumstances are teaching you bravery and patience?

What I am looking for is not out there; it is in me.
What do you find within?

People do not like to think. If one thinks, one must reach conclusions. Conclusions are not always pleasant.
Ponder an issue important to you; share your conclusions and explain if they are pleasant or not.

What we have once enjoyed we can never lose. All that we love deeply becomes a part of us.
What has become a part of you?

Believe, when you are most unhappy, that there is something for you to do in the world. So long as you can sweeten another's pain, life is not in vain.
Whose hurt might you help and how?

TEENS – It's Time to Grow Up

Helen Keller Quotes

FOR THE FACILITATOR

I. **Purpose**
   To personalize Helen Keller's wisdom and reach maximum potential.

II. **General Comments**
   Helen Keller rose above impediments in sight, speech and hearing, and she communicated crucial truths.

III. **Possible Activities**
   a. Before session photocopy the *Keller Quotes* handout and cut on the broken lines.
   b. Place the cut-out strips in a container face down.
   c. Remind teens how Helen Keller triumphed over disabilities and inspired people to reach their potentials.
   d. Explain they will be personalizing her words of wisdom.

   Impromptu Format
   - Teens take turns selecting a strip of paper, reading aloud the quote and question, and responding.
   - Teens pass the container of strips to the next peer when the current speaker finishes.
   - Emphasize there are no right or wrong answers and teens are invited to state what is true for them.
   - A teen may request peer help as needed.

   Prepare and Share Format
   - Teens select strips from the container and write their responses on the back or on a separate paper.
   - Encourage teens to share their responses.

   Individual Choice Format
   - Distribute the un-cut *Keller Quotes* handout to all teens.
   - Teens take turns choosing a few quotes to respond to aloud, or they write responses then share their work.

   e. After all quotes have been discussed, ask teens which concepts were most meaningful to them and why.

IV. **Enrichment Activities**
   a. Ask teens to apply other concepts conveyed by Helen Keller to their lives:
      - What small tasks can you accomplish as if they were great and noble?
      - What worthy purpose might you pursue?
      - In what ways have you lived in darkness and what light do you now see?
      - In what ways has trial or suffering strengthened you?
      - What beautiful things can be perceived only by your heart?
   b. Ask teens in teams, pairs, or individually, to compose their own quotes and questions.
      - Teens write them on strips of paper, and place into a container face down.
      - Teens take turns selecting a strip, reading and responding aloud.
   c. If possible, provide blindfolds and ear plugs for each student to experience Helen Keller's challenges.

Life Skills

Railroad Crossings

In most states passenger vehicles like buses must stop
before crossing the tracks.
In life it helps to stop and think, look at possible outcomes
and listen to opinions.

My *tracks* are (a challenging or dangerous situation I might decide to experience) … _____
_____
_____

The risks are (dangers and potential negative outcomes) …_____
_____
_____

The rewards are (growth opportunities and potential benefits) … _____
_____
_____

Next, listen to advice from around and within.
Label the speech balloons to show what is being said by different sources:

Parents/Caregivers   **A Trusted Adult**   **Friends**

                My Heart   **My Head**

TEENS – It's Time to Grow Up

Railroad Crossings

FOR THE FACILITATOR

I. **Purpose**
   To think before acting and consider risks and rewards; to listen to trusted advice and to one's inner voice.

II. **General Comments**
   Teens face opportunities for growth and dangerous temptations. They need to differentiate between healthy risks and real hazards.

III. **Possible Activities**
   a. Ask teens what it means when bells ring or whistles blow, red lights flash and a gate blocks entry onto railroad tracks.
   b. Ask teens to share times bells and whistles went off in their heads or a *still small voice* tried to warn them about someone or something.
   c. Encourage a discussion of potentially positive experiences that can be very scary.
   Possibilities:
   - A first date, starting a conversation with a prospective new friend.
   - A new school, class, club, extracurricular activity, or job.
   - Trying out for a team or entering a contest.
   d. Encourage a discussion of hazards that may appear appealing.
   Possibilities:
   - Alcohol and drugs.
   - Websites and social networking where teens can be victimized by bullying, sex, etc.
   - Gangs, bullying, gossiping.
   - Driving recklessly.
   e. Distribute the *Railroad Crossings* handout and allow time for completion.
   f. Encourage teens to share their responses.

IV. **Enrichment Activities**
   a. Ask teens to share examples and outcomes of times they listened to or ignored these warnings:
   - Their own common sense.
   - Advice from a trusted adult or good friend.
   - Their heads.
   - Their hearts.
   b. Encourage a discussion of healthy risks with seemingly negative outcomes, but ones that develop positive qualities in teens. If necessary provide the prompts below; possible teen responses are parenthesized:
   - A first date becomes the last (you gained social experience; you realized people don't always *click*; it's not your fault).
   - The conversation you started did not result in friendship (you learned you cannot control people's responses; at least you made the effort).
   - Peers at the new school are unfriendly (you learned you can survive; you will be more accepting of newcomers in the future).
   - A class, club, extracurricular activity or job is not what you expected, or you do not excel (you learned what is *not* for you, developed bravery by trying and perseverance if you persisted).
   - You were not selected for the team or you lost the contest (you learned from mistakes or might have received pointers from winners; you can decide to practice harder for next trial or to pursue a different challenge).

Life Skills

Rules of the Road BINGO

B 1-10	I 11-20	N 21-30	G 31-40	O 41-50
My emotional first aid kit includes…	I apply my brakes when…	A time I obeyed a caution light was…	I now have the green light to…	I yielded to something beyond my control when…
I drove ahead of my headlights when…	I cut someone off when…	A dead-end for me would be to…	I tend to tailgate a person by…	A pothole I can avoid is…
Double solid lines I will not cross are…	I'm driving uphill regarding…	A detour I need to consider is to…	I exceeded my speed limit when…	Distractions I need to ignore are…
I don't listen to passengers who…	My far bright headlights are showing…	I check my rear view mirror to…	I don't dwell on my rear view mirror because…	I'm driving in a traffic circle regarding…
I made a U-Turn when…	I went the wrong way on a one way street when…	I've parked too long in…	I expect and accept delays regarding…	My seatbelt is…

TEENS – It's Time to Grow Up

Rules of the Road BINGO

FOR THE FACILITATOR

I. **Purpose**

To apply safe driving concepts to life.

II. **General Comments**

Teens are motivated to learn to drive; related analogies heighten interest.

III. **Possible Activities**

BINGO Game
   a. Photocopy and distribute the *Rules of the Road BINGO* handout.
   b. Instruct teens to number the boxes randomly within the ranges of the numbers at the top of each column.
   c. Teens need to number differently from each other. Example, one may use even numbers, another odd numbers; others may do sequences like 1, 2, 3, 4, 5 or 10, 9, 8, 7, 6, etc. (Alternately, the facilitator or a volunteer may number the pages in advance).
   d. Facilitator calls one number per letter; teens with that number take turns sharing.
   e. Remind teens to answer figuratively; the questions apply to life, not driving. Examples:
      i. My emotional first aid kit includes coping skills.
      ii. I apply brakes when I think before I speak.
      iii. I drove ahead of my headlights when I rushed into a toxic relationship.
      iv. I tend to tailgate a person when I smother a partner by calling every 10 minutes.
      v. Distractions I need to ignore are negative self-talk, put-downs from peers.
      vi. I don't listen to passengers who tell me speed up.
      vii. I check my rear view mirror to learn from my past.
      viii. I don't dwell on my rear view mirror because I am focused on present and future growth.
      ix. I've parked too long in self-pity or in blaming others.
      x. My seatbelt is my faith, my self-respect.
   f. There are no right or wrong answers; teens tell what is true for them and color or mark the squares after they respond.
   g. If the same people keep having the numbers called, ask those who have not had a turn to pick the next number(s).
   h. Teens win by having marked off a diagonal, vertical or horizontal row.
   i. Continue playing as people win until all squares for everyone are marked (Black-Out BINGO).

   Write & Share Format
   a. Teens write their responses, then share as in the traditional BINGO Game.
   b. Alternately, teens take turns reading their responses aloud, starting with the squares from which they gained the most insight.

IV. **Enrichment Activities**
   a. White out all questions and photocopy or develop a BINGO page with blank squares.
   b. Photocopy, distribute, and ask teens individually, or in pairs or teams, to write in the blanks.
   c. Content should be related to growing up, or other teen topics.
   d. Photocopy their pages, distribute randomly, and ask teens to number them if you plan to use them for BINGO.
   e. Alternately, teens will take turns reading the questions aloud and responding.

Life Skills

GPS–GLOBAL POSITIONING SYSTEMS

Draw your road map on the back or write your driving directions below.

My destination is ...

My voice prompting directions tell me to ...

I'm advised to avoid ...

I could veer off track if ...

If I make a wrong turn, my automatic re-routing device will tell me to take these steps ...

TEENS – It's Time to Grow Up

GPS – GLOBAL POSITIONING SYSTEMS

FOR THE FACILITATOR

I. **Purpose**

   To compare driving to a destination to reaching a goal.

II. **General Comments**

   Driving and using electronics to map a route are grown-up activities. This session emphasizes self-direction and self-righting.

III. **Possible Activities**

   a. Ask for a show of hands from teens who have used or are familiar with internet map searches and global positioning systems.
   b. Write the sentences on the board as they are on the *Global Positioning Systems* handout.
   c. Ask teens to complete at least one exercise aloud as a volunteer writes on the board. Teens may decide on any positive *destination*. Example:
      - My destination is: to *improve my grades*.
      - My voice prompting directions tell me to *set aside "x" hours daily for study and homework; shut off the TV, radio and/or cell phone during study time; turn down extra hours of work on my volunteer or paid job; ask for peer help or tutoring if needed.*
      - I'm advised to avoid *constant social networking, late parties on school nights, friends who advise me to quit school.*
      - I could veer off track if *I put my social life ahead of my grades.*
      - If I make a wrong turn, my automatic re-routing device will tell me to take these steps: *cut down my hours at my job, add "x" minutes to my study time daily, ask my teachers for extra credit assignments.*
   d. Distribute the *Global Positioning Systems* handout and allow time for completion.
   e. Encourage teens to share their responses.

IV. **Enrichment Activities**

   a. Encourage a discussion about boats designed to right themselves when capsized.
   b. Ask how people can exhibit self-righting tendencies.
   c. Encourage teens to share instances where they survived difficult circumstances or changed their direction and behavior when headed toward disaster.
   d. Encourage a discussion of autopilots which guide aircraft or boats without human assistance.
   e. Ask teens to brainstorm activities they would like to be able to do automatically; a volunteer lists them on the board. Possibilities:
      - Use positive self-talk.
      - Use coping skills.
      - Forgive.
      - Persevere.
      - Use self discipline.
   f. Ask teens to brainstorm behaviors they do automatically but that they would like to stop; a volunteer lists them on the board. Possibilities:
      - Speak, text, e-mail in anger.
      - Seek negative attention.
      - Beat up on themselves.
      - Fight or flee stressful situations.

PARENTS, CARE-PROVIDERS, PARTNERS AND ROLE MODELS

A mentor is someone who sees more talent and ability within you than you see in yourself, and helps bring it out of you.
— BOB PROCTOR

Care-Provider Profiles .... page 45 ▶
Teens recognize how their parents' and/or care-providers' styles affect them and learn to meet their own needs as they mature. Parents and/or care-providers who play boss, coach, friend, acquaintance and genie are highlighted; broken-up parents, two who are not on the same page, caring for an impaired parent and other issues are addressed.

SUPERHEROES .... page 47 ▶
Teens identify and adopt traits of superheroes and human heroes: sacrifice, conviction, elasticity and others; teens recognize frailties and impulsivities in heroes or themselves and plan ways to change if warranted.

Romantic Partners .... page 49 ▶
Teens differentiate between immature crushes and meaningful partnerships by playing a game with categories: Love or Infatuation? Healthy Relationships and Warning Signs. Teens discuss the best and worst places to meet a partner, dating safety, whether love is blind, the likelihood of love at first sight and related topics.

Is It Love or Infatuation??? .... page 51 ▶
Teens recognize that jealousy, mistrust and pressure to compromise one's convictions characterize infatuation. Teens identify that mutual care, encouragement, understanding and trust are exhibited in love relationships.

Simon and the Leader .... page 53 ▶
Teens recall *Simon Says* and *Follow the Leader* and compare mindless mimicking to mature choices. Examples of Winner Leaders and Loser Leaders are discussed. Teens identify leadership qualities and how to become role models for younger siblings or others.

Parents, Care-Providers, Partners, and Role-Models

Care-Provider Profiles

The Boss: Strict rules, high demands, *Do it because I said so*; punishes disobedience.

The Coach: Defines rules; responds to needs and questions; nurtures and forgives.

The Friend: Allows self-regulation, avoids confrontation, lenient.

The Acquaintance: May provide food and shelter; emotionally detached.

The Genie: Gives me whatever I want; instant gratification.

Which profile best describes your primary childhood caregiver?
_____

How did your parents' or caregivers' style affect you?
_____
_____
_____
_____
_____
_____
_____
_____

As you mature, how do plan to be a parent to yourself?
_____
_____
_____
_____
_____
_____
_____
_____
_____
_____

TEENS – It's Time to Grow Up

Care-Provider Profiles

FOR THE FACILITATOR

I. **Purpose**

To recognize how teens' parents' or care-providers' styles affected them; to decide they can meet their own needs to a great extent as they mature.

To emphasize that no one, including the teens, will judge the caregivers; teens may decide to copy their styles or operate differently.

II. **General Comments**

Early childhood caregivers exert great influence; society often blames parents or caregivers for their teens' problems. As adolescents mature, they are more able to control their thoughts and behaviors and can learn from and grow beyond childhood experiences. Teens can decide which caregiver traits to adopt and which they do not want to perpetuate.

III. **Possible Activities**

1. **Group Discussion**
   a. List the care-provider profiles on the board and elicit qualities similar to the handout descriptions.
   b. Although caregivers may not fit a profile perfectly, and two parents may differ, ask teens to pick the profile most similar to their primary caregiver.
   c. Ask teens to divide into four teams and sit with peers who grew up under the same care-provider style.
   d. Distribute one *Care-Provider Profiles* handout per team; each team elects a writer who records their thoughts.
   e. Explain there are no right or wrong responses and that people growing up in the same type of households may answer very differently; they need not reach a consensus.
   f. Teams brainstorm; writers record; all re-convene; writers share their teams' ideas.
   g. Emphasize that young children are subject to caregivers' influence but mature teens and adults are more self-sufficient and self-directed; more able to self-parent or meet their own needs. Examples:
      - If caregivers were very demanding and punitive, teens can set standards for themselves and applaud progress not perfection.
      - If caregivers expected too little, teens can exert self-discipline, consider risks, rewards and consequences and recognize the world has requirements and restrictions.
      - If caregivers were absent or distant, teens can provide self-nurturing, self-acceptance, and realize it was not their fault that parents were inattentive or unavailable.

2. **Role-Play**
   a. Secretly assign the five profiles to five participants who sit at the front of the room.
   b. Audience (group) asks questions; the five volunteers respond according to their profile descriptions.
   c. Audience guesses the care-providers' roles. Example: A teen asks to stay out until three AM with a final exam the next day. **Boss** – *No way*; **Coach** – *Let's discuss the pros and cons*; **Friend** – *Sure, have fun*; **Acquaintance** – *I don't care*; **Genie** – *Here's some money for the date.*

IV. **Enrichment Activities**
   a. Ask teens whether their caregivers acted similarly or had different styles. Ask how this affected them.
   b. Ask teens to describe their experiences with a single parent and/or bouncing back and forth between split-up parents with different styles.
   c. Encourage a discussion regarding children who parent or care for a sick, disabled or addicted caregiver and how this has affected them.
   d. Encourage teens to discuss the pros and cons of taking major responsibility for younger siblings.
   e. If any teens are themselves parents, and if they are willing to respond, ask them to share the pros and cons of being a teen mom or dad.

Parents, Care-Providers, Partners, and Role-Models

SUPERHEROES

Fill in the blank boxes.

Superheroes	Traits I Admire	Ways I Can Demonstrate those Traits
Example: *Spider Man*	*Brainy but real (struggles with feeling inadequate and lonely), tries to do right, clings to surfaces, knows that with power comes responsibility.*	*Do my best in school, focus on my strengths not my doubts, stick to tasks, use my abilities to improve things at home and school.*
Human Heroes	**Traits I Admire**	**Ways I Can Demonstrate those Traits**
Example: *Teacher*	*Funny, understanding, fair to everyone and helpful.*	*Laugh at myself, do my best to be fair to everyone, be a good listener when friends share problems, help others.*

SUPERHEROES

FOR THE FACILITATOR

I. **Purpose**
   To identify and adopt traits of superheroes and human heroes.

II. **General Comments**
   Children and adolescents admire fantasy figures and real people. Modeling heroes' attributes helps teens develop positive qualities.

III. **Possible Activities**
   a. If possible, display an internet picture of Superman or other superhero.
   b. Ask teens to brainstorm fantasy figures; a volunteer lists them on the board.
   c. Encourage a discussion regarding qualities the characters exhibit, especially those qualities that teens can possess.
      Example: Superman is powerful yet humble, respects human life, stands his ground.
   d. Ask teens to identify categories of human heroes (family members, teachers, athletes, humanitarians).
   e. Distribute the *Superheroes* handout and allow time for completion.
   f. Encourage teens to share their responses.

IV. **Enrichment Activities**
   a. Ask teens to elaborate on aspects of heroism and apply them to their lives. Prompts:
      - Sacrifice – What will you give up for the sake of something of higher value?
      - Dedication – What course of action will you bind yourself to?
      - Valor – In what current combat do you need bravery?
      - Conviction – What unshakable belief will guide and drive you?
      - Enthusiasm – What positive act are you eager to participate in?
      - Elasticity – How can you spring back quickly from a set-back?
   b. Ask teens to discuss the frailties of their superheroes or possible human weaknesses. Prompts:
      - Arrogance – How have you felt contempt toward or disregarded people who are less capable than you?
      - Misuse of power – How have you wasted your abilities by doing harm or by failing to help?
      - Impulsivity – How have you acted on sudden urges you later regretted?
   c. If teens reveal frailties, ask them what steps they took, or plan to take, to change.
   d. Create Your Own Superhero
      - (For Fun) – Individuals, teams, or the entire group can create a superhero by brainstorming a name, appearance, special powers, personality, the human counterpart, (like Clark Kent for Superman), a catchphrase for the character, friends, foes, weapons, vehicle, frailties, etc. Teens may enjoy making posters or writing stories or poetry about the superhero.
      - (For additional learning) – Teens may wish to create and/or identify a human superhero describing name, gender, age, attributes, weaknesses, social system surrounding the hero, career, family, etc. They may enjoy performing a short mock video, writing a story line or poem showing the hero's struggles and accomplishments.

Parents, Care-Providers, Partners, and Role-Models

Romantic Partners

Love or Infatuation?
1. In the beginning, what usually ignites a relationship? (physical attraction).
2. Initially, do people put their best foot forward, or show their real self, and why? (portray their best self, want the partner's approval, fear their more human side may be rejected).
3. What does it mean to have the right partner in terms of your social group? (to be with someone cute and cool without considering their inner qualities).
4. How do relationships change in a helpful way after the initial rosy glow? (people focus on inner traits, mutual understanding and caring).
5. What is emotional closeness? (share thoughts, feelings, hopes, fears; listen to and support each other).
6. What is commitment? (promise to stick together through thick and thin).
7. Why do teen relationships often end? (inadequate time and attention; interest in dating many people; go separate ways or to different colleges, grow apart due to different interests or goals).
8. What are benefits of having loved and lost? (learned how to give and take, identified positive personal qualities and what you might want to change; found out what to look for and avoid in a partner).

Healthy Relationships
1. Give an example of honoring a partner's boundaries (do not urge the person to do something they are uncomfortable doing).
2. Give an example of emotional support (let someone cry on your shoulder or celebrate a triumph together).
3. Give an example of equality in a relationship (take turns selecting a movie or whose friends to hang out with; no one chases the other or plays hard to get).
4. How can partners maintain separate identities? (spend some time apart to see other friends, do favorite activities, develop new talents, maintain responsibilities at home).
5. Give an example of good communication (I feel… statements, express concerns, ask for what you want or need, listen actively, reflect each other's feelings, respect that *no* means *no*).
6. What does it mean to smother or hover? (needs constant in person or electronic contact).
7. How is conflict resolved? (share feelings, brainstorm ideas, compromise; no violence or put-downs).
8. How do partners show they trust each other? (believe each other, give room for individual pursuits).

Warning Signs
1. Describe four types of abuse (physical harm, verbal insults, sexual force, taking or conning someone out of money).
2. How does a person isolate a partner? (insists they avoid friends, family, support groups, etc.)
3. Give an example of over-control (makes the partner quit an activity or class; wants to know every move; dictates how to think, speak, act, dress; pushes a person to make decisions contrary to the person's conscience).
4. Give an example of manipulation (person pouts to get their way or flirts to make partner jealous).
5. What is a characteristic of a narcissistic partner? (vain, self-absorbed, conceited).
6. How do dangerous or detrimental partners initially present themselves? (may be good-looking, smooth talking, use flattery, appear kind and caring).
7. What might be part of an unhealthy partner's history? (cruelty to animals, fire-setting, violence, alcohol or drugs).
8. What should you do if you are in an unhealthy relationship? (admit it, talk to a supportive person, make a clean break, then allow yourself to cry; give yourself time to heal, do what you enjoy, keep busy; don't rush into a rebound relationship; seek therapy if you are depressed).

TEENS – It's Time to Grow Up

Romantic Partners

FOR THE FACILITATOR

I. **Purpose**

To differentiate between immature crushes and meaningful partnerships.

To decide to depart from destructive romances and seek healthy relationships.

II. **General Comments**

Romance is a major part of growing up. Teens will heighten their awareness of relational red flags by answering game questions.

III. **Possible Activities**

a. Ask teens what is most important to them; they may soon mention dating and relationships.
b. Explain they will play a game regarding romance.
c. Write the topics on the board: Love or Infatuation? Healthy Relationships, Warning Signs.
d. Ask a volunteer to play Love Quest Questioner; provide the teen with the *Romantic Partners* handout. Advise Questioner to NOT read the parenthesized responses until after the peer answers.
e. Teens take turns selecting a category; Questioner reads the question, the teen responds.
f. Teens state what is true for them and may ask peers for assistance.
g. There are no definite answers; the parenthesized phrases are merely examples.
h. Questioner crosses off questions as they are asked.
i. After the questions and answers, write the following on the board; encourage discussion and debate:

> *Do I love you because you are beautiful?*
> *Or are you beautiful because I love you?*
> ~Richard Rogers and Oscar Hammerstein II, *Cinderella*.

IV. **Enrichment Activities**

a. Teens in teams or as a group may brainstorm the following or related topics; a volunteer writes their responses on paper or the board.
b. Possible places to meet a partner.
   - Might include school, work, house of worship, volunteer site, club or organization.
c. Dating safety.
   - Double date, or stay with a group of friends, until you know the person better.
   - Avoid isolated environments; tell parents where you'll be and with whom; keep cell phone charged and at arm's reach.
   - Have a code word in case you need to call for help.
d. Is love blind? Why or why not? (Open to interpretation).
e. Is love at first sight possible? Why or why not? (Open to interpretation).
f. What are the differences between puppy love and adult dog devotion?
   - Puppies show playful affection, are fickle with short attention spans, seem to love everyone, run from person to person; they are easy to manipulate with treats as rewards.
   - Adult dogs sense your moods, comfort you when you cry, give unconditional love, warn you of danger, defend you against foes, and you need not look your best around them! They understand many commands but don't always obey.

Parents, Care-Providers, Partners, and Role-Models

 ## Is It Love or Infatuation???

Place an L next to the statements that apply to a loving relationship and an I next to those that apply to infatuation. Place a B next to statements that apply to both.

1. _____ Wants what is best for the other person.

2. _____ Bases the relationship on what the other person looks like.

3. _____ Bases decisions on what is good today and in the future.

4. _____ Enjoys spending time with the other person.

5. _____ Is concerned with "living in the moment".

6. _____ Understands when the other person cannot hang out because he or she has made prior commitments to be somewhere else.

7. _____ Pressures the other person to take steps he or she isn't ready to take.

8. _____ Trusts the other person.

9. _____ Encourages the other person to use all of his or her talents in life.

10. _____ Suggests that the other person behave in a dishonest way.

11. _____ Likes to spend time with people who are important to the other person.

12. _____ Only talks to the person when no one else is around or on instant message.

13. _____ Is jealous of other friendships.

14. _____ Has pictures of the person on his or her social media page to show off the relationship.

15. _____ Brags about things that happened between the two of them to make him or her look cool.

Contributed by Annette Damien, MS PPS

TEENS – It's Time to Grow Up

Is It Love or Infatuation???

FOR THE FACILITATOR

I. **Purpose**

   To differentiate between love and infatuation.

II. **General Comments**

   Romantic relationships greatly impact teens. Often, initial feelings of attraction can be confused for feelings of "love". Although infatuation may lead to the development of a deeper relationship, relationships that continue to be based on infatuation over time exhibit characteristics of jealousy, mistrust, and pressure to compromise one's convictions. In this activity, teens will contrast infatuation's selfishness and superficiality with love's mutual care, encouragement and trust.

III. **Possible Activities**

   a. Ask teens *What does it mean to be in love with love?* (To be in a romance is the priority, not the person; many teens want a boy/girlfriend to fit in or for status).
   b. Encourage a discussion about romantic themes in songs, movies, television shows and literature.
   c. Write on the board *Infatuation* and ask its meaning (addictive attraction; may not last).
   d. Write *Love* on the board and ask its meaning (deep affection and caring; may be platonic between friends or romantic between partners).
   e. Distribute the *Is It Love or Infatuation???* handout.
   f. Allow time for teens to complete the questions.
   g. Encourage teens to share and substantiate their responses. Possible answers:
      1. Love – True love always puts the other person first.
      2. Infatuation – focuses on physical appearance.
      3. Love – looks to the future, not only living in the moment.
      4. Both – we can enjoy spending time with those we love or those we are infatuated with.
      5. Infatuation – based on the here and now, no thought of future plans or consequences.
      6. Love – Key word here is *understands*.
      7. Infatuation – Key word here is *pressures*.
      8. Love – Love is based on trust.
      9. Love – In a loving relationship, partners encourage each other to live to their full potential and share their gifts with the world.
      10. Infatuation – Acts of dishonesty or that ask another to compromise their convictions are not those based on love.
      11. Love – In a loving relationship, you grow to also care for and love those that are important to each other.
      12. Infatuation – A relationship that is kept secret or private is not based on love.
      13. Infatuation – Key word is *jealousy*.
      14. Both – Although the word "show off" is used here, we can feel proud of a loving relationship. We may also brag about an infatuation. Without knowing the motive behind the action, we must say it could be either.
      15. Infatuation – The difference between #14 and #15 is the motive– to make "him or her look cool."

IV. **Enrichment Activities**

   a. Encourage teens to discuss differences between love and infatuation regarding flaws, duration of the relationship, sex, problems and conflict, levels of security and commitment, etc.
   b. Ask teens to share their experiences with love and infatuation.

Parents, Care-Providers, Partners, and Role-Models

Simon and the Leader

I listened to Senseless Simon and did this:

_____

The outcome:

_____

I listened to Savvy Simon and did this:

_____

The outcome:

_____

Follow the Leader

Who am I following? (name code) _____

When? _____

What am I doing? _____

_____

_____

Why? _____

_____

_____

Where am I going? _____

_____

_____

TEENS – It's Time to Grow Up

Simon and the Leader
FOR THE FACILITATOR

I. **Purpose**
   To decide to listen to wise advice and to follow positive role models.

II. **General Comments**
   Teens recall childhood games and compare mindless mimicking to mature choices.

III. **Possible Activities**
   a. Before session coach two teens to role play a *Simon Says* game.
   b. Simon portrays the actions and verbally commands: *Simon says hands on head, Simon says hands on shoulders, hands on hips*; the player performs all the actions; Simon says, *you lost!*
   c. The teens perform for the peer audience, then Simon asks *why did the player lose?* (Because the words Simon says did not precede *hands on hips*).
   d. Encourage a discussion about children being taught to do as they are told versus teens who give in to peer pressure, think for themselves, or rebel against advice from authority figures.
   e. Ask teens to describe *Follow the Leader*, (do as the leader does or you're out).
   f. Ask teens to brainstorm *Loser Leaders* and *Winner Leaders* while a peer lists their ideas on the board. Possibilities:

Loser Leaders	*Winner Leaders*
Drinking or drugging peers	People in the public eye who overcome obstacles
Gang leaders	Peace promoters
Bullies	Main characters in literature and film who beat the odds
Students who encourage others to cheat	Humanitarians
Celebrities who disobey the law	Family, friends, teachers with understanding and compassion
Sports heroes who dope	Athletes who win fairly

   g. Distribute the *Simon and the Leader* handout and allow time for completion.
   h. Encourage teens to share their response

IV. **Enrichment Activities**
   a. Ask teens to identify leadership qualities they exhibit or want to develop. Possibilities:
      - **Honesty** – tell the truth, admit errors.
      - **Vision and Passion** – see what *can* be done, go for it, enlist experts, share your mental picture.
      - **Competence** – let people see the positive results of your actions, learn from mistakes.
      - **Wisdom** – choose a learning lifestyle, read, study strategies to reach your goals, ask questions and listen.
      - **Dedication** – do what's needed and others may follow your example.
      - **Fairness** – find the facts, don't jump to conclusions, extend to everyone the dignity they deserve.
      - **Expectations** – You get what you expect; plan on people doing their best and thank them.
      - **Humor** – don't take yourself too seriously, see the funny side of situations.
   b. Encourage a discussion regarding when teens might be leaders; for whom they might serve as role models. Possibilities:
      - Younger siblings.
      - Younger children they tutor, coach or babysit.
      - Peers who need to surmount similar hurdles.

HOME, SCHOOL AND WORK 4

The place where you made your stand never mattered.
Only that you were there... and still on your feet.
— STEPHEN KING

Role Renovations .... page 57 ▶
Through a mingle and match game teens link dysfunctional family roles with their descriptions. Teens identify each position's pros and cons and collaborate about renovations, i.e., the hero might seek progress not perfection; the scapegoat might be accountable if wrong and assertive when right.

Charity Begins .... page 59 ▶
Teens consider ways to be kind and compassionate closest to home; teens then brainstorm ways to personalize this John Wycliffe quote: *Charity should begin at himself.*

Yearbook .... page 61 ▶
Teens apply yearbook concepts to life: qualities that make one likely to succeed, extracurricular benefits, lessons, mental photos, future visions, hidden talents, survey subjects, and others. Through debates teens articulate the pros and cons of controversial categories (cutest couple, best dressed, etc.) and articles (sexual issues, teen parents, etc.).

Are You Ready? .... page 63 ▶
Through a skit or mock video teens portray Helen Keller's breakthrough at the water pump. Teens consider the Gautama Buddha quotation *When the student is ready the teacher will appear,* and discover their readiness, human and non-human teachers, who they might teach and how.

The Three R's .... page 65 ▶
Through a teacher-student game teens link reading, writing and math to life, literally and figuratively. Teens apply other R-words (resourceful, rational, reflective, etc.) to adulthood and are encouraged to write real-life letters to newspapers, school administrators, legislators and others whom they may influence.

(Continued on the next page)

HOME, SCHOOL AND WORK

(Continued)

My Challenges .... page 67 ▶

Teens discuss websites and they tell what works for them. Teens write about their own challenges and reinforce ideas, actions, inner strengths and wisdom. At the facilitator's discretion and if teens are willing, their comments are shared aloud or photocopied into booklets to help each other.

Fix 10 .... page 69 ▶

Through skits or mock videos or storytelling, teens meet The Woeful Worker, Not So Honest *and observe* The Unimpressive Interview. *Teens identify poor work habits, unproductive traits and behaviors, and then they substitute positive practices. Teens are encouraged to write their own scenarios and correct detrimental habits.*

Home, School and Work

Role Renovations

Roles	Descriptions
Enabler	I cover for, and bail out, the person with the problem.
Hero	My achievements make the family look good to others.
Scapegoat	I get blamed, get in trouble and get attention.
Lost Child	I'm a loner; I steer clear from the chaos.
Mascot	I'm the class clown; my humor relieves tension.
Dysfunction	Family members' lives revolve around it.
Common Goal	To escape pain or reality or gain self-worth.
Secret	All members keep it; problems flourish in its darkness.

Role _____

Pros _____
_____
_____

Cons _____
_____
_____

Renovations _____
_____
_____

TEENS – It's Time to Grow Up

Role Renovations

FOR THE FACILITATOR

I. **Purpose**

To identify roles which often develop in dysfunctional families, their positive and negative features.

II. **General Comments**

Teens mingle, find their role or description match, then collaborate about recovery. Problem, secret and common goal are included as they have roles in dysfunction. The handout may also be used as an individual activity.

III. **Possible Activities**

a. If available show a stuffed animal and ask its role in a sports team (mascot).
b. Explain that in some families teens might be a mascot or play a different role.

Match and Mingle Game Format
- Before session photocopy and cut the *Role Renovations* handout; make one set of roles and one set of descriptions and enough copies of the bottom portion for each pair of participants or larger team.
- Place the roles and descriptions face down in a container; ideally sixteen teens will each select a slip.
- If there are more than sixteen present, others will observe initially, then become team members.
- If fewer than sixteen are present, put that number of matching roles and descriptions in the container, proceed as follows, then start over with the remaining roles and descriptions.
- Teens mingle and match up with the appropriate role or description.
- Verify correct matches: they are correctly paired on the uncut handout which is the answer key.
- Distribute the bottom portion to each pair of teens; additional teens team up with the pairs.
- Pairs or teams collaborate; a writer records responses; all reconvene and share their ideas. Examples:

Role	Pros	Cons	Renovations
Enabler	Assumes responsibility.	Rescues; must be needed or in control to feel worthy.	Lets others face consequences.
Hero	Works hard.	Neglects own needs.	Enjoys the process; seek progress not perfection.
Scapegoat	Admits faults.	Sees self as *bad*; lives out the image.	Be accountable if wrong; be assertive when right.
Lost Child	Appreciates solitude.	Keeps people at an emotional arm's length.	Open up to trusted helpers; let yourself love.
Mascot	Humorous	Fakes funniness; freezes feelings.	Allow pain to surface; use humor, but not as a mask.
Secret	Honors confidentiality.	Makes it worse.	Share it and ask for help.
Dysfunction	Fosters change.	Dominates and entraps.	Recognize it; seek recovery.
Common Goal	Brings about collaboration.	Leads to rigid responses.	Use each role's strengths; break away from the cons.

Individual Format

Distribute the uncut handout; teens identify their roles, complete the questions and share their responses.

IV. **Enrichment Activities**

Encourage teens to identify the role they usually play and how they will break the unhealthy pattern.

Home, School and Work

Charity Begins...

Charity begins at home. ~ Sir Thomas Browne

1. Animals
2. Children
3. Disabilities
4. Diseases
5. Education
6. Environment
7. Equality
8. Homelessness
9. Hunger
10. Literacy
11. Mental Health
12. Peace
13. Physical Health
14. Spirituality/Religion
15. Senior Citizens
16. Veterans

Charity should begin at himself. ~ John Wycliffe

1	2	3	4	5	6	7	8
9	10	11	12	13	14	15	16

TEENS – It's Time to Grow Up

Charity Begins...

FOR THE FACILITATOR

I. Purpose

To be kind, compassionate and helpful first to oneself, then to family and friends.

II. General Comments

Accolades abound when people publicly give; authentic altruism begins behind closed doors.

III. Possible Activities

a. Before session photocopy the *Charity Begins ...* handout and cut the numbered squares on the broken lines; place face down in random order in a container.
b. Write on the board *Charity begins ...* and ask teens to finish the sentence (accept all responses).
c. Ask teens to explain how charity begins at home and to define *charity* beyond donating money: time, effort, understanding, etc.
d. Ask a teen to play *Charity Chairperson*; give the handout to the chairperson who reads items corresponding to numbers.
e. Teens take turns pulling a number; chairperson reads the corresponding charitable cause; teens describe how to demonstrate related charitable acts close to home.
f. There are no right or wrong responses; teens may ask peers for help. Possibilities:
 1. Animals (adopt a shelter animal; pet sit or walk friends' or neighbors' dogs).
 2. Children (babysit younger siblings willingly; act as a good role model).
 3. Disabilities (help a relative with an impairment; prevent home injuries through safety precautions).
 4. Diseases (help ill family and friends; promote nutrition, exercise, frequent handwashing; etc.).
 5. Education (tutor siblings or other children; teach older adults computer skills).
 6. Environment (clean the house, do yard work, pick up litter, recycle, dispose properly).
 7. Equality (respect the rights of family and friends; demonstrate open-mindedness through actions).
 8. Homelessness (offer part of your allowance or earnings to family for rent or mortgage).
 9. Hunger (help buy and prepare family meals; pack lunches; give leftovers to a friend or neighbor).
 10. Literacy (read bedtime stories to younger siblings; donate books to family and friends).
 11. Mental health (ask family members how they feel; show empathy; give extra attention and love).
 12. Peace (resolve family conflicts through compromise; pick your battles; be flexible).
 13. Physical health (grocery shop for healthy foods; play outdoor games with younger siblings).
 14. Spirituality/Religion (see the good in family members; have hope and encourage others to have hope).
 15. Senior citizens (run errands for grandparents; call or visit elderly relatives).
 16. Veterans (write to relatives in the military; thank a service person when you see one).

IV. Enrichment Activities

a. Write on the board **Charity should begin at himself.** ~ John Wycliffe
b. Ask teens to brainstorm its meaning; a volunteer records their ideas. Possibilities:
 • Give yourself positive messages.
 • Praise your efforts regardless of outcomes.
 • Forgive yourself.
 • Examine what you can do differently now that you know more.
 • Take care of your physical and emotional needs.
 • Ask for and accept help.
 • Give yourself gifts (needed items, pats on the back, enjoyable activities, coping skills).

Home, School and Work

Yearbook

1. **Most Likely to Succeed:** List at least five qualities that contribute to success and share how you plan to display or develop them.

2. **Acronyms:** Use each letter of your name or your initials to begin a word or phrase about your plans.

   Example - Tom might write:

   T – To myself I'll be true and pursue piano.

   O – Or compose lyrics and tunes.

   M – Music makes my heart sing.

3. **What extracurricular activities** have you been in and what did you learn about yourself, others, life? Or, if you declined involvement, share why and your thoughts about wanting to change.

4. **Describe your role model:** teacher, staff member, peer, family member or famous person; include at least five qualities you plan to emulate.

5. **What have you learned** from watching or participating in sports about victory, defeat, sportsmanship, leadership, sharing responsibility and glory, etc.?

6. **Yearbooks have lots of photos.** Draw or describe your most positive mental picture from your past and then for your finest vision for your future.

7. **Share your thoughts about a hobby or hidden talent** you would like to develop into a career and how you might proceed.

8. **Some yearbooks include surveys.** Share and substantiate your opinion on a controversial subject.

9. **Depict (draw, use symbols or cartoons)** or describe your five most meaningful experiences within the last year. Share how they fit into your book of life.

10. **Debates** – Discuss the pros and cons of including these categories in a yearbook:
    - Most Likely to Succeed
    - Best Looking
    - Best Athlete
    - Brainiest
    - Most Popular
    - Cutest Couple
    - Most Likely to Join a Sorority or Fraternity
    - Class Clown
    - Most Ethical
    - Most Compassionate
    - Most Honest
    - Best Role Model
    - Best Dressed

TEENS – It's Time to Grow Up

Yearbook

FOR THE FACILITATOR

I. **Purpose**

To consider yearbook components, form and express opinions and apply related concepts to life.

II. **General Comments**

Yearbooks emphasize reflections on experiences; teens think about their past, lessons learned, and future.

III. **Possible Activities**

a. If available display a yearbook; ask teens about their experiences with yearbooks.
b. Distribute the *Yearbook* handout.
c. Ask teens to select an item from numbers 1-9, or to choose an issue to debate about from number 10.
d. Allow time for teens who selected an item from numbers 1-9 to complete their work.
e. While peers complete their work, debaters pick topics and pair up; one takes pro and the other takes con.
f. Debaters make brief notes and prepare for their performance.
g. Teens who responded to items 1-9 take turns sharing their responses.
h. Debaters then speak: up to two minutes each, one minute for rebuttals.
   Concepts they might address:

Category	Pros – Gains	Cons – Outcomes
Most Likely to Succeed	Positive reinforcement	People not picked may feel like losers.
Best Looking	Recognition	External emphasis.
Best Athlete	Acknowledgment	Ignores those who try and are good team players.
Brainiest	Respect	Only one of many top students is applauded.
Most Popular	Recognition	May be for superficial or fleeting reasons.
Cutest Couple	Attention	Romance may be short-lived.
Most Likely to Join a Sorority or Fraternity	Rewards an outgoing personality	Some join even though they can't afford it and because they think they'll make fast friends.
Class Clown	Appreciation for humor	May tend to overuse humor or mask feelings.
Most Ethical	Acknowledgment of an often ignored attribute	Ethics aren't always evident; the most ethical acts may not be seen.
Most Compassionate	Gratitude	Compassionate people may not be identifiable; they may perform random acts of kindness.
Most Honest	Credit given for an often ignored virtue	Honest acts may be done in private, like not looking at someone's text or e-mail message.
Best Role Model	Appreciation	Many great role models are left out.
Best Dressed	Compliments and acceptance	People find out that clothes alone do not make the person.

IV. **Enrichment Activities**

Encourage teens to discuss topics some yearbooks might include, whether and why they are or are not appropriate:

- An interview with a gay student who came out of the closet.
- An article about a couple who have a baby.
- Features about former graduates and where they are now, what they are doing, etc.
- An article about a person who started a charity.

Home, School and Work

Are You Ready? Script

Characters: Narrator; Helen Keller as a child; Teacher – Ann Sullivan

Props: Empty mug or cup, unbreakable doll or a picture of a doll, small amount of water in another cup, wastebasket.

Narrator reads the bold text a loud; characters portray the parenthesized actions silently.

~ The Miracle Worker ~

An illness left Helen without vision or hearing.
(Helen closes eyes and places hands over ears).

The teacher, Ann, tried to link words with objects, like doll and mug, using finger spelling.
(Ann puts a mug and doll in Helen's hand and forms letters on the other palm).

Helen did not understand and was so frustrated that she broke her doll.
(Helen throws down the doll or its picture).

Then at the water pump, Ann finger-spelled w-a-t-e-r onto one of Helen's hands. She poured water over the other.
(Teacher spells w-a-t-e-r onto child's hand and pours a little water over the other; position wastebasket under the hand to catch the water.)

Helen understood.
(Helen jumps up and down, thumbs up, with happy facial expression).

Then she demanded to know the names of other objects.
(Helen runs around touching three or four items in the room, a chair, table or desk, pen or paper. Ann finger spells each onto Helen's hand and Helen finger spells back onto teacher's hand to show comprehension).

Helen later explained,
The touch of her hand did more than illuminate the pathway of a clouded mind; it literally emancipated a soul.

Narrator asks peers:

- At what moment was Helen ready to learn that objects had names?
  (When water was poured on her hand).

- Consider this quotation:
  When the student is ready the teacher will appear. ~ Gautama Buddha

- What are you ready to learn?

- Are our teachers always actually human?

- Who or what might be your teacher?

- What other *teachers* might appear?

- What has touched you and opened your heart?

- Who might you teach and how?

TEENS – It's Time to Grow Up

Are You Ready?

FOR THE FACILITATOR

I. Purpose
   To welcome human and non-human teachers at intellectual and heartfelt levels.

II. General Comments
   Teens need to see the lessons in front of their eyes, and reach out to teach others.

III. Possible Activities
   a. Before session:
      - Make three photocopies of the *Are You Ready?* handout (script) and gather props.
      - For dramatic effects, real water may be poured over Helen's hand (with wastebasket underneath).
      - Give three volunteers the script; they rehearse out of sight and out of earshot of peers.
   b. When session begins:
      - Tell the audience they will see a mock video about Helen Keller and Ann Sullivan.
      - Narrator reads aloud as the two actors pantomime their parts.
      - Everyone applauds the performance; actors take their seats; narrator remains at front of the room.
   c. Narrator reads the follow-up questions and peers take turns responding. Examples:
      - Teens personalize what they are ready to learn and from whom; (honesty, responsibility, empathy, enthusiasm, insight, better study habits, a new skill, etc. from specific role models).
      - Lessons need not be from human teachers. Lessons are learned from experience, adversity, trial and error.
   d. Ask teens how they'll know when they are ready and willing to absorb each lesson in front of them (be open-minded, learn from others and from mistakes and see problems as learning experiences).
   e. If possible, show the movie or a clip from *The Miracle Worker*.

IV. Enrichment Activities
   Read aloud the following statements and questions; possible responses are parenthesized:
   - Ann Sullivan had childhood problems with illness, poor eyesight, mom's death, dad's abuse and abandonment. How did this help her to be a good teacher? (Compassionate, understood struggles).
   - What might your challenges prepare you to do? (Individualized responses).
   - Ann studied how to teach children with sight and hearing problems. In her valedictorian speech she said, *Duty bids us to go forth into active life…and set ourselves to find our especial part*. What active life do you plan and what might be your special part? (Individualized responses).
   - Later, Ann found schools to help Helen, accompanied her and helped her through Radcliff College. What does this tell us about Ann? (She did not try to be everything to her student).
   - In what area of your life do you need to give up some control or allow others to share the credit? (Individualized responses).
   - While helping Helen write her autobiography, Ann and the editor fell in love and married. The couple continued to help Helen. What does this say about Ann? (Loyalty).
   - To what person and/or value do you want to be loyal? (Individualized responses).
   - Many years later Ann died; Helen was holding her hand. Why is this significant? (Helen remained dedicated to her teacher and the breakthrough with the water involved their hand contact).
   - Helen became an author, lecturer and political activist. She founded organizations devoted to health, vision, nutrition, equality and civil liberties. What do you think motivated her? (Her own adversity made her want to help others).
   - How might you use your experiences to improve others' lives? (Join a political or social action organization, volunteer for a cause, use literary, artistic, music, theatrical or other talents to convey your message; become involved in science or medical research or service to decrease disease, etc.)

Home, School and Work

The Three R's

Reading

1. What might motivate a person to read?   *(Texts, e-mails, instant messages from friends; articles or books about teams, rock stars; web sites about topics of interest, curiosity, career information).*
2. What are some social benefits of reading?   *(Become an expert that peers go to for info; share humor, riddles and jokes; engage in conversations about the material with other people).*
3. What are some personal benefits of reading?   *(Thrills and chills without being in danger; travel to other times and places; solve mysteries; read about characters with your issues; self-development).*
4. How might reading expand your intellectual or humanitarian horizons?   *(Develop new interests; find a cause you believe in; improve your memory, concentration and creativity).*
5. How might reading blogs and customer reviews help you?   *(Find other opinions; consider pros and cons of products before buying).*
6. In what situation are you starting to read between the lines?   *(Person shares insights).*
7. What helps you read a person's emotions?   *(Facial expression and body language).*
8. Finish this sentence: *Read my lips…*   *(Person states a strong opinion or promise).*

wRiting

1. What might motivate a person to write?   *(Express strong opinions in letters to the editor or to a legislator; social networking).*
2. What are the benefits of writing in a diary or journaling?   *(Clarify thoughts and feelings; see problems differently; find creative solutions; develop and document a story; get things off your chest; gain insight into disagreements; track progress).*
3. What might you write if you want to make a decision?   *(Options; a list of pros and cons for each).*
4. What is the benefit of writing fifteen minutes daily about anything using free flowing stream of consciousness? *(Hidden thoughts may emerge or topics you will decide to think more about).*
5. How might your writing help others?   *(They may learn from your experiences; you may entertain them with stories or make them think about an issue; you may touch them with a poem).*
6. What bad experience do you need to let go of but remember the lesson learned?   *(Person shares the situation and its significance).*
7. What should you not put in writing, except in your journal?   *(Anything written in anger; gossip).*
8. **We write to taste life twice.** ~ Anais Nin. What experience would you like to relive or reflect upon?   *(Person shares the event and its meaning).*

aRithmetic

1. How might math help with buying a car?   *(Compare prices, insurance, whether to buy or lease).*
2. How might math help you start a business?   *(Calculate expenses, salaries, profits, losses).*
3. How might math help you at home?   *(Calculate areas for wall covering, flooring and repair costs).*
4. How might math help you manage money?   *(Calculate savings, investments, taxes, credit costs).*
5. What might you subtract to streamline your life?   *(Person shares what they will eliminate and why).*
6. What might you add to improve your life?   *(Person shares the trait or activity).*
7. In what situation do the facts not add up and how might you correct it?   *(Person shares the circumstance and action plan).*
8. What do you have in abundance that you might divide among others to multiply their joy?   *(Person shares a tangible possession or intangible trait).*

The Three R's

FOR THE FACILITATOR

I. Purpose
To see the value of these subjects in everyday teen as well as future life.

II. General Comments
The game incorporates educational concepts with life lessons.

III. Possible Activities
a. Write on the board *ABCD...* and *2+2=4*.
b. Ask teens what is represented (alphabet for reading and writing and an addition example for mathematics).
c. Explain that teens will apply these basics to teen and future life.
d. Select a teacher from the group.
e. Give *The Three R's* handout to the teen *teacher* who will read questions aloud.
f. Remind the *teacher* to avoid revealing the parenthesized responses until after the students speak.
g. Teens (*students*) take turns selecting a category (reading, writing or arithmetic) and responding.
h. There are no right or wrong answers; possibilities are parenthesized.

IV. Enrichment Activities
a. Explain that in the past reading, writing and math were the basics.
Write on the board three new R's: *Rigor, Relevance* and *Relationships*.
b. Ask teens to apply these three R's to their education by asking the following questions:
Rigor: Are your lessons difficult enough to challenge you? Explain.
Relevance: Share examples of how you connect new knowledge to your life experiences.
Relationships: In what ways do you develop meaningful relationships with peers and allies in education? How might you form more positive alliances?
c. Ask teens to brainstorm attributes that start with R and apply them to teen and adult life.
Possibilities:
- Responsible
- Respectful
- Resilient
- Resourceful
- Righteous
- Receptive
- Reflective
- Ready
- Rational
- Reasonable

d. Encourage a discussion about the effects of technology on reading, writing and math (Internet research, e-books; texting, blogging; calculators, etc.) and how these improve or weaken skills.
e. Ask teens how reading biographies might help them (learn how successful people overcame adversity, tried and failed before it all worked out, took several jobs before they found their niche, encountered criticism, rebounded after a setback, dealt with challenges).
f. Provide adult-like real life writing opportunities. Teens might prepare and disseminate:
- Letters to the president, governor, senators, congressmen and legislators regarding laws, social justice, etc.
- Letters to the school board or superintendant regarding problems and solutions.
- Articles for the school newspaper, yearbook pieces, or letters to the local newspaper's editor.
- Petitions (written and signatures gathered) to improve the community, to start new programs or services.

g. Encourage teens to calculate costs of a graduation trip or compare college or vocational school costs and benefits.

Home, School and Work

My Challenges

Consider your three most meaningful challenges and write how you deal with them – or not. Your ideas are private unless you want to share.
It's best to dig deeply for your own issues, but if you need ideas consider this list.

Assert my rights	Face fear	Help others	Remain calm
Bounce back	Follow good role-models	Inspire	Respond to authority
Change	Forgive myself	Lead	Stay true to myself
Communicate	Go through grief	Learn from mistakes	Survive my past
Compromise	Grow	Love myself	Sustain my faith
Contribute	Handle parental pressure	Manage conflict	Think positively
Deal with a break up	Handle partner pressure	Meet goals	Thrive
Decide	Handle peer pressure	Overcome obstacles	Treat people
Express my feelings	Help myself	Prioritize	Uplift my mood

My Most Meaningful Challenges

1. How I … _____
_____
_____
_____
_____
_____
_____

2. How I … _____
_____
_____
_____
_____
_____
_____

3. How I … _____
_____
_____
_____
_____
_____
_____

TEENS – It's Time to Grow Up

My Challenges
FOR THE FACILITATOR

I. Purpose
To reinforce ideas and actions and reveal inner strengths and wisdom.

II. General Comments
Teens like to post opinions and see how others solve problems.

III. Possible Activities
a. Write on the board *Experience is the best teacher*; ask teens to apply the quote to what they have learned.
b. Encourage teens to discuss their experiences with websites where people share how they deal with issues.
c. Explain that teens will write about how they handled or might handle an important challenge or how they struggle with an issue.
d. Emphasize that the writing is personal, private and to be shared only if they wish.
e. Write *How I …* on the board and ask teens for examples they would like to share or learn about (How I … meet people, plan for a first date, etc.)
f. Distribute the *My Challenges* handout; a volunteer reads aloud the statements in the box.
g. Encourage teens to come up with their own ideas; they may refer to the list if necessary.
h. Ask teens to write on notebook paper or the back of the handout.
i. Direct teens to first state the challenge for numbers 1, 2 and 3 and then elaborate.
j. Encourage teens to include thoughts and actions they used or use to help themselves or what they think might help.
k. Allow time for completion.
l. Encourage teens who want to share to read their page aloud and receive peer feedback.

IV. Enrichment Activities
a. Encourage teens to read current articles and books to learn from other teens.
b. If appropriate for your setting and for teens who are willing, photocopy and compile the writings anonymously or with names and distribute among the group; teens will learn from each other by reading their booklets.
c. Teens who are not effectively dealing with challenges may request and receive peer suggestions.

Home, School and Work

Fix 10

Scenarios to read aloud or role play as audience notes ten ways to improve:

The Woeful Worker

1. Stays up until 3:00 AM the night before an exam.
2. Pushes the snooze button three times.
3. Appears sleepy; puts on clothes from a heap on the floor.
4. No time for breakfast; grabs a soda and candy bar.
5. Clocks in at work at 8:56 AM but was supposed to start at 8:00 AM.
6. Works energetically at first due to a sugar high, then crashes and naps on the job.
7. The boss asks about sluggishness; the worker says, *"It's none of your business."*
8. The boss asks worker to clean up a restroom; worker says, *"It's not in my job description."*
9. A customer waits until the worker finishes a text message.
10. Worker tells the boss about a co-worker who came back five minutes late from lunch.

The Unimpressive Interview

1. Candidate slouches, looking sloppy, shirt half out and half in, a piece of paper stuck to shoe.
2. Shakes employer's hand either too roughly or like a limp dishcloth.
3. Chews gum.
4. Looks around the room, daydreams, asks employer to repeat the first question twice.
5. Rambles at length in the response as eyes glance around the room.
6. Uses familiar and slang terms; calls the employer *dude*.
7. Boasts about increasing sales 500% at last job.
8. Tells employer *If you don't hire me I'll be homeless and starve.*
9. When asked to give an example of how the candidate handled a complaint at a past job, the candidate brags, *A customer complained that the food was too cold. I said, "Take it home and microwave it." The customer left immediately but forgot to take the food. I ate it.*
10. Candidate does not say *thank you* at the end of the interview.

Not So Honest

1. Worker arrives at work late; tells employer, *"I was here on time but was in the restroom."*
2. The boss reprimands the worker for a mistake on a report; worker blames it on someone else.
3. The boss asks about a task that was to be done yesterday; worker says, *"You never told me that."*
4. A co-worker asks for help; worker answers, *"I'm too busy."*
5. Worker takes a long lunch break to meet someone at the bank; worker tells the boss, *"I got stuck in traffic."*
6. Co-worker lent worker fifty dollars at the bank; worker promises, *"I'll pay you back double tomorrow."* Doesn't.
7. Worker takes twenty dollars at the end of shift; worker explains, *"Another worker stole it."*
8. Worker's pay check has an error, three extra hours of pay, and worker plans how to spend it.
9. Worker is fired and tells family, *"I was laid off because of the poor economy."*
10. Worker lies about a co-worker's honesty hoping to get that position.

TEENS – It's Time to Grow Up

Fix 10

FOR THE FACILITATOR

I. **Purpose**

To identify poor work habits, personal traits and behaviors and substitute positive practices.

II. **General Comments**

Through mock videos and/or story telling, teens collaborate to right what's wrong.

III. **Possible Activities**
   a. Before session photocopy the *Fix 10* handout and cut on the broken lines.
   b. Ask teens how they find and keep jobs (want ads, applications, interviews and good work habits).
   c. Explain that teens will watch mock videos or hear stories, then find and fix poor work habits.

Story Telling Format

Three story tellers alternately read scenarios aloud and prompt peers to brainstorm better work habits.

Mock Video Format
- Divide teens into three teams; give each team copies of one of the scenarios.
- Teammates sit together, if possible out of sight and hearing distance from other teams.
- Teams may act out the story with speaking roles or a narrator may read while others pantomime.
- Teams decide who will direct, act, narrate; extra team members advise and add ideas.
- After brief rehearsals, reconvene; teams perform skits; audience takes notes about wrongdoing.
- After each skit, teens brainstorm positive habits and traits to replace the poor ones. Examples:

The Woeful Worker
1. Get enough sleep.
2. Wake up on time.
3. Shower, brush teeth, wear clean clothes.
4. Eat a nourishing breakfast.
5. Be on time.
6. Keep a steady pace.
7. Answer or apologize appropriately.
8. Follow instructions.
9. Text only during scheduled breaks.
10. Focus on one's own work habits.

The Unimpressive Interview
1. Dress neatly.
2. Shake hands firmly.
3. Discard gum before interview.
4. Make eye contact and listen.
5. Answer concisely.
6. Use professional titles and language.
7. Tell the truth.
8. Appear motivated but not desperate.
9. Show sensitivity to customer needs.
10. Always say *thank you* at the end of an interview.

Not So Honest
1. Take responsibility if late.
2. Admit mistakes.
3. Do what is asked; no excuses.
4. Help co-workers when possible.
5. Return from lunch on time.
6. Keep promises.
7. Never steal or blame others.
8. Be honest if overpaid.
9. Tell family the truth and learn from mistakes.
10. Do not try to manipulate situations.

IV. **Enrichment Activities**

Encourage teens to write and share their own scenarios; peers identify and correct unproductive habits.

TANGIBLE AND INTANGIBLE 5

> It is the heart that makes a man rich.
> He is rich according to what he is,
> not according to what he has.
> — Henry Ward Beecher

Bigger and Better .... page 73 ▶

Through a team game teens compete for bigger and better objects. Teens recognize that stuff cannot provide self-worth or satisfaction and consider ways to contribute to society rather than to consume. Teens identify ways they play Bigger and Better *with peers, how the media entices buyers and the connection between increased esteem and decreased materialism.*

Budget Breakdown .... page 75 ▶

Through a romantic role-play concerning credit and a team budget activity (without dollar amounts) teens identify sources of income and ways to spend, save and share. Teens may elect to jointly raise funds for an organization or a cause.

Expense Exchange .... page 77 ▶

Teens consider what to let go materially and behaviorally to have funds for priorities and to be rich regarding peace of mind, self-determination and other intangibles. Teens decide whether specific pursuits are worth the cost in terms of lifestyle and well-being.

Alphabet Soup .... page 79 ▶

Through a game, teens personalize mature virtues and concepts.
Examples:
  Authenticity: How can you let more of the real you shine through?
  Indomitable: About what issue will you not bend, flinch, crouch or give in and why?
  Universality: Share an issue you thought was yours alone, but now know others experience it.
  Zeal: What idea, cause or goal energizes and enthuses you and how will you keep it alive?

YOUR MOVE .... page 81 ▶

Through narrated scenarios with teen actors who pantomime, teens ponder ethical dilemmas and discuss mature moves. Situations involve school, work, parents, applications, accidents, rivalry, mistakes and other circumstances.

Tangible and Intangible

Bigger and Better

What did your team have that was bigger and better?

What did the other team have?

Who won?

Materialism:

How do you and your friends play Bigger and Better?

_____
_____
_____
_____

How does the media entice you?

_____
_____
_____
_____

What is the connection between self-esteem and wanting the newest gadget or the best brand?

_____
_____
_____
_____

Bigger and Better

FOR THE FACILITATOR

I. Purpose
To decrease materialism in teens; to consider being contributors to society versus excessive consumers.

II. General Comments
Teens recognize that stuff cannot provide self-worth or satisfaction.

III. Possible Activities
a. Divide teens into two teams; teammates sit together, ideally a distance away from opponents.
b. Give each team a small item with little value like a paper clip.
c. Teams find one item amongst themselves that is bigger and better then the paper clip and what might be bigger and better than the opposing team's item, (teams might produce a cell phone, designer tennis shoe, etc.).
d. The team with the bigger and better object wins the game.
e. Emphasize that in life bigger and better is not always what matters.
f. Distribute one *Bigger and Better* handout to each team; a writer for each team reads the questions.
g. Teammates brainstorm and the writers record their responses.
h. Teams reconvene and team writers share their team's ideas. Possible responses:
   - Teens play *Bigger and Better* by buying the latest electronics, designer clothes.
   - The media entices via TV commercials, Internet sites, music videos, that promote consumerism.
   - The connection with self-esteem involves seeking status and self-worth through material items.
   - Satisfaction with self and life leads to less materialism; valuable character traits, pursuing your passion and contributing to the world are more fulfilling than possessions.
i. Ask teens how being bored might lead to buying binges, (watch too many TV commercials or spend too much time meandering through the mall).
j. Ask teens how being scheduled to the max might cause them to indulge in *retail therapy*.

IV. Enrichment Activities
a. Encourage a discussion about how adolescent attitudes affect adult spending. Examples:
   - Teens who work and save might become more productive and sensible adults than those whose parents gave them everything.
   - Teens who save money might be less likely to buy now and pay later as adults.
   - Teens who live within a budget may live within their means as adults.
b. Ask teens to differentiate between wants and needs. Examples:
   - Needs involve food, shelter, health care, education.
   - Wants involve gourmet food, the newest fad in shoes and the most prestigious universities.

Tangible and Intangible

Budget Breakdown

Circle your team's person:

| 16-year-old high school student. | 20-year-old college student. | 20-year-old working person. | 26-year-old career person, married with a child. |

Income Source(s) _____
_____
_____
_____
_____
_____

Spend: _____
_____
_____
_____
_____
_____

Save: _____
_____
_____
_____
_____
_____

Share: _____
_____
_____
_____
_____
_____

TEENS – It's Time to Grow Up

Budget Breakdown

FOR THE FACILITATOR

I. **Purpose**

To create a theoretical budget incorporating income, spending, saving and sharing.

II. **General Comments**

Credit card concepts and money management are crucial in young adulthood.

III. **Possible Activities**

a. Before session recruit three teens to role play a *first date* at a restaurant; coach them regarding the scenario; they rehearse in advance and then will perform.
b. Three teens perform the scenario - the server, the first dating partner, the second dating partner:
   - Dating partners comment about the delicious meal and look lovingly into each other's eyes.
   - The server brings the check; the first dating partner grabs it, looks wide-eyed, and gives it to the second dating partner.
   - The second dating partner looks at the bill with shock and says *I thought you would pay*.
   - The first dating partner says *I don't have enough money*.
   - Audience claps and role players take their seats.
c. Ask audience what two problems were portrayed (not knowing who would pay; too little money).
d. Ask how the problems could be prevented (decide ahead to split the bill; have adequate funds).
e. Elicit that if the partners were savvy about money they could have avoided embarrassment.
f. Discuss the benefits of budgets and ask teens about their experiences with money management.
g. Explain that each team will develop a budget for a theoretical person; no math required.
h. Distribute the *Budget Breakdown* handout; teens select their person from the four choices.
i. Teens sit close to teammates who chose the same person; a writer elicits and records their ideas.
j. Remind teams to brainstorm sources of income, all possible expenditures, what their person is saving for, how their person manages money and cuts costs.
k. Point out that *Share* involves charitable donations of money or fund-raising.
l. Allow time for teams to complete their budgets; all reconvene; writers read aloud their budgets.
m. Encourage a discussion regarding credit cards and money management. Examples to elicit:
   - If credit cards are used, pay in full each month or more than the minimum payment.
   - It's more rewarding to save for an item than to pay bills after an object's newness wears off.
   - Beware of credit card cash back and rewards; these amounts are far less than the interest.
   - Consider a debit or pre-paid credit card.
   - Use cash when possible and carry only enough cash for planned purchases.
   - Spend only paper money; save all coins; they'll add up over time.
   - Think for a week before a major purchase; comparison shop; avoid impulsive buying.
   - Save receipts. Write down everything you buy including gum, coffee and sodas for a week.
   - Track *needs* versus *wants*; note what can be cut (restaurant food, movie theaters).
   - Shop thrift stores, garage and yard sales for bargains; sell or donate what you no longer need.
   - Savings may be for college, a house, a car; also set aside about three to six months of living expenses in case you lose your job; learn about Certificates of Deposit and investing.
   - Have money automatically deducted from your paycheck into a retirement account.
   - Sharing can be donating to a cause; opportunities include faith-based funds, disaster relief, the environment, health, human services.
   - Check each charity's financial and track records.

IV. **Enrichment Activities**

Encourage teens to collaborate about an organization to which they might jointly donate time or money; they need not give cash but might collect cans or plastics for recycling or raise funds through a car wash.

Tangible and Intangible

Expense Exchange

Apply Henry David Thoreau's words to you:
A man is rich in proportion to the number of things he can afford to let alone.

> Example: I can let alone ... *an expensive sports event that impresses my date.*
> To be rich regarding ... *my college savings and a partner who likes me for me.*

I can let alone ... _____

_____

_____

To be rich regarding ... _____

_____

_____

The price of anything is the amount of life you exchange for it.

> Example: I have exchanged ... *time with family and genuine friends.*
> For ... *drugs, alcohol and partying with acquaintances.*
> The price is ... *not worth it.*
> Because ... *my emotions and grades went downhill, I have damaged relationships with friends and let my family down.*

I have exchanged ... _____

_____

_____

For ... _____

_____

_____

The price is ... _____

_____

_____

Because ... _____

_____

_____

Expense Exchange

FOR THE FACILITATOR

I. **Purpose**

   To decide what to let go materially and behaviorally to have funds for priorities and to be rich emotionally.

   To determine whether specific pursuits are worth the cost in terms of lifestyle and wellbeing.

II. **General Comments**

   Teens are urged by advertisers to buy big or they are influenced by peers and society to be someone they are not.

III. **Possible Activities**

   a. Write on the board *Budget* and head two columns *Income* and *Expenses*.
   b. Ask teens how budgets work (determine your earnings and spend less).
   c. Ask teens what to do if spending exceeds income (cut costs or make more money).
   d. Ask teens what *rich* means to them (a lot of money, fancy cars and homes).
   e. Ask about other ways to be rich (have love, health, peace of mind; pursue a passion).
   f. Ask teens to consider what a workaholic gives up for worldly success (family time, relaxation).
   g. Ask teens to consider the price paid for what dominates their lives and whether it is worth it.
   h. Distribute the *Expense Exchange* handout; teens read aloud the quotes and sentence starters.
   i. Allow time for completion then encourage teens to share their responses. Possibilities:

I can let alone …	To be rich regarding …
Expensive electronics, costly clothes or concerts.	Funds for college or a car, or to help others.
Drugs and alcohol.	Finances, physical and mental health.
People pleasing or popularity seeking.	Self-determination.
Negative peer pressure to cheat or bully.	Self-respect for upholding my values.

Note that exchanges may or may not be worth the cost. Examples:

I have exchanged …	For …	The price is …	Because …
Face-to-face or voice contact.	Excessive texts, e-mails and blogs.	Not worth it.	I lost some personal social skills.
Rest and recreation.	Perfectionism.	Not worth it.	I have no peace.
Some social events.	School work.	Worth it.	College acceptance requires good grades.
My dream career.	A job with better pay.	Not worth it.	My work-life is awful.
My dream career.	A job with better pay.	Worth it.	It will help me financially and experience-wise to pursue my dream.

IV. **Enrichment Activities**

   Encourage a discussion about help for teens who say they can't give up possessions or behaviors.
   Examples:

   - A person who needs the newest devices may need counseling to improve self-worth.
   - People addicted to substances may seek help from a physician and support groups.
   - People-pleasers need to know that real and trusted friends will accept them for their true and unique traits.
   - People influenced by negative peers need assertiveness skills and new friends.

Tangible and Intangible ▶

Alphabet Soup

A – **Authenticity** – How can you let more of the real you shine through?

B – **Belief** – In what or whom do you need to have more faith and trust?

C – **Cooperation** – With whom might you accomplish more than you would alone and how?

D – **Diligence** – In what do you need to do your absolute best and how?

E – **Ethical** – In what ways are you decent or honorable?

F – **Foresight** – What future benefits or troubles do you see regarding a prospective plan of action?

G – **Gentleness** – In what situation might a softer approach work better for you and how?

H – **Hope** – About what do you have or need hope and what are your expectations?

I – **Indomitable** – About what issue will you not bend, flinch, crouch, or give in and why?

J – **Justice** – In what ways are you treating people as you want to be treated?

K – **Kindness** – To whom can you show more kindness and how?

L – **Loyalty** – How can you stand up for a person in your life or for an ideal you believe in?

M – **Moderation** – About what are you very enthused and how can you not be swept away?

N – **Non-violence** – In what ways are you handling anger or potential aggressive tendencies?

O – **Order** – What are your top priorities and how do you organize your days to encompass them?

P – **Patience** – About what have you done all you can and how can you now calmly wait?

Q – **Quick-witted** – How do you use your humor to make people feel good?

R – **Respectful** – How can you treat others with dignity or honor the rules at home, school and community?

S – **Soul-searching** – What do you need to think hard about and why?

T – **Thankfulness** – Share gratitude for a thought, feeling, action, lesson, or a little thing in your life.

U – **Universality** – Share about an issue you thought was yours alone, but now know others experience it.

V – **Victory** – What obstacle will you overcome and how?

W – **Wisdom** – Based on your knowledge and experience, what decision do you need to make?

X – **X-rated** – What person, place, thing or thought will you not allow yourself to experience and why?

Y – **Yes** – What do you say Yes to that you feel good about?

Z – **Zeal** – What idea, cause, or goal energizes and enthuses you and how will you keep it alive?

TEENS – It's Time to Grow Up

Alphabet Soup
FOR THE FACILITATOR

A	B	C	D	E	F	G	H	I	J	K	L	M
N	O	P	Q	R	S	T	U	V	W	X	Y	Z

I. Purpose
To identify mature virtues and concepts and apply them to life.

II. General Comments
Teens discuss attributes and ideas in a game format.

III. Possible Activities
a. Before session write the letters of the alphabet in random order on the board inside a large circle; scatter the letters to resemble pasta in alphabet soup.
b. Cut out the letters of the alphabet (above) on the broken lines and place in a container, if possible a bowl.
c. Ask a volunteer to play game show host and another to play the assistant.
d. The game show host sits at the front of the room; the assistant stands at the board.
e. The assistant holds the bowl of letters and an eraser for the board.
f. The host has a copy of the *Alphabet Soup* handout.
g. Remind teens they may have eaten alphabet soup earlier as a child but will now *consume* the letters in an adult way.
h. Teens take turns picking a letter from the bowl; host reads the corresponding word and question; teens respond according to what is true for them.
i. A teen may ask a peer to answer the question as it applies to that person's life.
j. The assistant erases each letter from the circle on the board as it is used.
k. The group collaboratively wins when all letters are erased.
l. Optionally, all teens may win a prize, (a healthy treat, being allowed to socialize for five minutes, or a *No Homework Tonight* slip for a particular class, etc. as appropriate for the setting).

IV. Enrichment Activities
a. Draw a circle on the board.
b. Volunteers take turns thinking of a virtue-related word and applying it to their lives.
c. Teens write the first letter of their word after they share.
d. The group collaboratively wins when they fill the bowl with the twenty six letters of the alphabet.

Tangible and Intangible ▶

YOUR MOVE

**The narrator reads the scenes aloud; when possible, actors pantomime.
Action stops when the narrator says, *"Your move."* The actors and the audience discuss options.**

1. You arrived at your sandwich shop job late and customers are already lined up. You see the expiration date on tuna salad was yesterday. You have no time to make fresh salad and no one to help you. Your first customer orders tuna on whole wheat. Your move.

2. You live with your parents. You're out with friends and see one of your parents hugging your other parent's best friend. Your move.

3. You race from school to work, then study until after midnight. Your college applications ask about your extracurricular and volunteer activities during the last two years; you have had none. Your move.

4. You are driving home in a hurry. A neighbor struggles down the street in a wheelchair with lots of groceries. If you provide a ride you'll have to load and unload the wheelchair and groceries. The neighbor does not see you. Your move.

5. You turn your wheel too sharply as you back out of a parking space. You dent the car next to you. No one observed the incident. Your move.

6. You are asked out by a person you really like but you have to babysit. The person asks to visit you after the children go to bed. You have been told to have no with you when you babysit. Because your schedules conflict, you will not see the person for at least a month. Your move.

7. Your dating partner left you for your former best friend. Your former friend is now accused of stealing twenty dollars dropped in the hall. You witnessed another person pick up the money. Your move.

8. You drop a valuable vase at the store where you work. It shatters into pieces. No one sees you do it and there are many co-workers in your department who could have done it. Your move.

9. You plan to break up with your dating partner. Your birthday is in three days. You know your partner has an expensive gift for you, something you really want. Your move.

10. You started a different school and your new friends are rich. They want to hang out at your house and your parents will welcome them. You think your house is not as nice as theirs. Your move.

TEENS – It's Time to Grow Up

Your Move
FOR THE FACILITATOR

I. **Purpose**
   To ponder ethical dilemmas and discuss mature moves.

II. **General Comments**
   Scenarios are more memorable when enacted; teens learn through active involvement and collaboration.

III. **Possible Activities**
   a. Write on the board *Talk is cheap* and ask teens to interpret (it's easy to say but harder to do the right thing).
   b. Explain that teens will discuss how they might act in sticky situations.
   c. Make one photocopy of the Your Move handout; only the person playing narrator sees the scenario.
   d. Teens take turns as narrator and actor(s).
   e. Each narrator asks for the appropriate number of volunteer actors.
   f. The narrator reads aloud as actors portray the scenario without words.
   g. Numbers 6, 9 and 10 do not require acting; the narrator simply reads those scenes.
   h. The action stops when narrator says "Your move"; actors and audience discuss what they might do.

   Ethical considerations teens might discuss:
   1. Public health and food safety comes before the worker's time limits and convenience.
   2. To question the parent who seems to be unfaithful is more upfront rather than to mention it to the other parent.
   3. The temptation is to lie on the application, but honesty is required.
   4. Depending on the situation, to help others is often more important than one's own agenda
   5. The temptation is to sneak away, but accountability is admirable.
   6. The temptation is to violate rules, but trustworthy teens say, "No" to the visit.
   7. Revenge seems sweet but the bigger person reveals truth even if it saves a rival.
   8. The responsible person owns up to the mishap, apologizes and offers to pay for it.
   9. The temptation is to break up after the birthday; the fair-minded person gives up the gift.
   10. The authentic teen lets people see the house and knows genuine friends do not judge.

IV. **Enrichment Activities**
   a. Ask teens to share ethical dilemmas they experienced and how they responded.
   b. Ask teens individually or in teams to write brief scenarios, read them aloud, and elicit peer feedback.

THE JOURNEY 6 TO MATURITY

Don't judge each day by the harvest you reap,
but by the seeds that you plant.
— Robert Louis Stevenson

Dirt or Soil .... page 85 ▶

By comparing dirt with soil teens differentiate between perceived manure and profitable fertilizer. Teens note their dirt or difficulties; for each they state a nutrient – lesson learned or strength developed. Teens identify ways to weed out hostile internal environments like negative self-talk.

Bloomer Mixer .... page 87 ▶

Through a mixer or individualized puzzle, teens match famous late bloomers with their one sentence biographies. Teens learn that talents not yet evident may emerge. Teens personalize lessons (how to overcome adversity, it's ok to be different, etc.) and identify what helps late bloomers flourish.

Rites and Responsibilities .... page 89 ▶

Teens depict and describe their separation, transition and reincorporation stages from adolescence to adulthood; they link rights with responsibilities. Teens discuss cultural rites of passage, and give opinions about wilderness programs and other experiences.

Freeze Tag .... page 91 ▶

By viewing a pantomime, teens recognize when frozen or stuck and identify internal and external ways to mobilize. Teens define what tagged them, how they are stagnated regarding thoughts, feelings, actions or inactions, and where they will go and what they will do when freed.

GLADIATOR OR GOPHER? .... page 93 ▶

Through a game teens adopt the positive aspects of the gladiator mentality and avoid dangerous extremes. Real-life situations are provided; teens identify how they might react as a foolish gladiator, gopher, or wise gladiator.

Am I There Yet? .... page 95 ▶

Through a game, teens stand under Agree or Disagree wall labels and recognize signs of immaturity and maturity. A few of the concepts: invincibility, ways one's behavior affects others, helplessness, blame, entitlement, empathy, assertion, unfairness, compromise and interdependence.

(Continued on the reverse page)

THE JOURNEY TO MATURITY

(Continued)

Perspectives (It's All How You Look at It) .... page 97 ▶

Teens look back, within and forward prompted by a person, place, thing or idea that has always been part of their lives. Teens note how age and perspective affect experiences and emotions. They also practice stating negative and positive interpretations of events.

Continuums .... page 99 ▶

Teens acquire self-knowledge about traits and values by looking at extremes and middle-of-the-road options. On horizontal lines or scales, teens show where they are, where they want to be, and how to get there based on peer feedback.

Sex Sense .... page 101 ▶

Through thought-provoking questions, teens (in private written format) describe how sexual decisions affect their lives. Teens are neither advised nor judged. They are encouraged to ponder their three most meaningful issues from a list of possibilities: abstinence, safe sex, pregnancy, sexually transmitted diseases, same sex attraction, gender identity, abusive partners, rape recovery, how faith and/or values affect sexuality and other topics.

Dirt or Soil

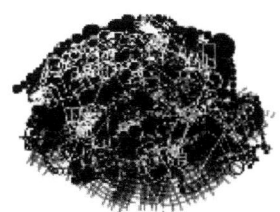

Dirt: A substance that spoils the cleanness of somebody or something; dust, filth, grime.

Soil: A medium in which growth and development take place.

Imagine and then draw or describe yourself as a seed, covered and surrounded by dirt. Show what seems to smother you and may even smell bad!	Imagine and then draw or describe yourself emerging from the muck (smelling like a rose?). Show the nutrients or benefits you derived from the fertilizer.

My sun is (sources of illumination and inspiration) …

TEENS – It's Time to Grow Up

Dirt or Soil

FOR THE FACILITATOR

I. Purpose
To compare seed emergence to personal growth and development.

II. General Comments
Teens will recognize that what looks like dirt is soil that develops maturity and character within.

III. Possible Activities
a. If possible display a seed and soil, or pictures of plants emerging from the earth.
b. Ask teens why animal manure is used (feces has rich nutrients needed for growth).
c. Ask teens to describe dirt in a human's environment (problems, unpleasant experiences, challenges, perceived failures, mistakes, detrimental relationships, etc.).
d. Ask how what seems to disgust or demoralize can promote positive traits (learn from experiences and become stronger).
e. Distribute the *Dirt or Soil* handout and read the definitions of dirt and soil aloud.
f. Allow time for completion.
g. Encourage teens to share their responses.

Examples of dirt: difficulties	Examples of soil: lessons learned and strengths developed
• Hostile environments at home or school where people insult or bully.	• Self-worth is an inside job; ignore negative messages.
• A break up or being outcast by peers.	• Wisdom about people and relationships.
• Failure to pass a class.	• Recognition of personal value regardless of grades.
• A physical or mental disability.	• Your identity is more than a diagnosis.
• Social humiliation.	• Ability to rise above what people may think.
• Target of abuse.	• Realization that survival is possible.
• Mistakes, blunders.	• Self-forgiveness, willingness to make restitution.

• Examples of the sun or sources of inspiration and illumination: faith, spirituality, nature, the arts, literature; supportive people and positive role models, etc.

IV. Enrichment Activities
a. Encourage a discussion of hostile internal environments and ways to weed them out. Possibilities:
   • Negative self-talk (positive thought substitutions).
   • Anxiety (talk, write, draw, exercise, meditate, use guided imagery or visualization).
   • Guilt (admit mistakes, try to make amends).
   • Resentment (strive to let go and move on; forgive for your own sake).
   • Sense of inadequacy (do not compare yourself with others, find and focus on your strengths).
   • Loneliness (help others through volunteer work or random acts of kindness).
b. Ask teens what it means to grow where you're planted. Possibilities:
   • You can grow in a small plot of land – you don't need a big house, car, or bankroll to flourish.
   • You can push through hardened dirt or frost – motivation and perseverance raise you up.
   • Like a seed, you have within you the potential to become the winner you were born to be.

Bloomer Mixer

J.K. Rowling	British, single mom wrote her first Harry Potter book in her 30s.
Angelo Siciciliano (Charles Atlas)	He had sand thrown in face, was bullied, a 97 lb. weakling, achieved body building fame in his late 20s.
Brendan Gleeson	Mad Eye Mooney in Harry Potter films, Irish actor who began his career in his 30s.
Colonel Harland Sanders	Founded Kentucky Fried Chicken restaurant chain in his 60s.
Charles Perrault	Wrote *Tales from Mother Goose* including *Cinderella* and *Tom Thumb* in his late 60s.
Abraham (Bram) Stoker	Horror fiction writer, created *Dracula* in his 50s.
Leo Fender	Automated the manufacture of the electric guitar in his 40s; developed precision bass and amplifiers.
Ian Fleming	English spy thriller author, began creating James Bond (007) adventures in his 40s.
Ray Kroc	Milkshake machine salesman, joined McDonald's in his 50s, built the successful fast food chain.
Jules Verne	French author started writing science fiction like *Journey to the Center of the Earth* in his 30s.

TEENS – It's Time to Grow Up

Bloomer Mixer
FOR THE FACILITATOR

I. **Purpose**
   To know that talents not yet evident may emerge; teens may be late bloomers.

II. **General Comments**
   Teens learn they can become more than they are at the moment.

III. **Possible Activities**
   a. Before session photocopy the *Bloomer Mixer* handout and cut on the dotted lines, either one set of cut-outs for the Mixer Format or a set for each teen for the Puzzle Format.
   b. Write *child prodigy* on the board; ask for examples, (Mozart - music, Bobby Fischer - chess).
   c. Explain that some people's talents show up early; others are late bloomers.

   Mixer Format
   - Scramble the cut-outs and ask teens to select one.
   - Explain that some people received a name; others received a description of accomplishments.
   - Teens mix and mingle, walking around the room to find their *match*.
   - The original *Bloomer Mixer* handout is the answer key for the facilitator to determine if the teens are properly paired.
   - After teens with names find teens with their corresponding descriptions, all take their seats.
   - Pairs take turns going to the front of the room, sharing their identities and accomplishments.

   Puzzle Format
   - Scramble each set of cut-outs and distribute one pile to each teen.
   - Teens lay the cut-outs on their desks and then put the matching descriptions next to the names.
   - The uncut page is the answer key for facilitator to determine if teens have matched correctly.
   - Teens share their matches to ensure all have the correct answers.

   Conclusions for either the mixer or puzzle format to relate to teens in the group.
   Elicit these ideas:
   - Don't be discouraged if you are not the best athlete, academic or artistic performer.
   - Your strengths and talents may be ready to emerge or may develop later.
   - If you are an early bloomer, it is still important to work hard (in addition to using your inborn talent).
   - Many late bloomers face the same problems others do; then find their own way to bloom.
   - It's OK to be different, or a deep thinker.
   - Academics aren't everything (some thought Edison wasn't very bright).
   - Many surmounted poverty, abuse, problems at home, or people who discouraged them.

IV. **Enrichment Activities**
   Ask teens to brainstorm what helps late bloomers flourish.
   Examples:
   - Be open to inner sparks: find what you love to do, care greatly about an issue or stand up to an atrocity you want stopped.
   - Reflect on what others see in you: empathy, encouragement, a skill. How might you use these?
   - Compare yourself to no one but see strengths in others that you might adapt to your needs.
   - There are many ways to attack obstacles: rise above, go through, find a new route; don't give up.
   - A book, poem, performance, piece of art or music, nature etc. may speak to you.
   - A jam may jolt you, a mistake may make you decide to do things differently.
   - A missed opportunity might make you more alert to future possibilities.
   - Praise your efforts to find your passion; if it hides – seek.
   - Enjoy your journey. It is a process of self-discovery. Be patient; you're not finished yet.

Rites and Responsibilities

Separation is detaching from an earlier point in life. Depict and/or describe your separation process.

[   ]

Transition means you are in between two stages. Depict and/or describe how this is for you.

[   ]

Reincorporation means entering adulthood with a new identity. Depict and/or describe what you foresee.

[   ]

TEENS – It's Time to Grow Up

Rites and Responsibilities

FOR THE FACILITATOR

I. **Purpose**
   To identify the transition from child to adult: the rites of passage.

II. **General Comments**
   Across cultures, adolescent to adulthood rituals may differ, but the stages are generally universal.

III. **Possible Activities**
   a. If available display a driver's license and a voting ballot and ask teens what the items have in common (they signify adulthood).
   b. Encourage a discussion about rites of passage in other cultures (shaving young men's heads; sending them into the wilderness to survive unassisted, etc.).
   c. Ask about coming of age in this country (graduation, voting, induction into the military, getting a job, going to college).
   d. Distribute the *Rites and Responsibilities* handout. Teens draw, use symbols, cartoons, or words to convey thoughts.
      - Ideally teens will use large paper and colored markers, crayons, paint.
      - Ideally the project will be completed in three separate but consecutive sessions.
      - The handout may be used *as is*, with only pen or pencil, and the three boxes may be completed in one session if necessary.
   e. Encourage teens to share their work.
      - Examples of separation involve leaving the comforts and security of home, less parental control, growing away from childhood friends, separating from allowances to after school jobs.
      - Examples of transition involve being torn between immature interests and mature responsibilities; teens might draw themselves being pulled in opposite directions or at a brink or crossing a chasm.
      - Examples of reincorporation involve career and family roles or character traits they plan to exemplify. As adults, they might also feel more *put together* within.
   f. Conclude with a discussion of rights and responsibilities inherent in adulthood. Examples:

Rights	Responsibilities
To choose career, college or other training.	To put forth best efforts at school or work.
To drive a vehicle.	To obey safety and traffic rules.
To date and seek a mate.	To treat people well, never to abuse nor exploit.
To form political views and social consciousness.	To be an informed voter; to devote time to a cause.

IV. **Enrichment Activities**
   Ask teens to address these topics:
   - Some cultures inflict physical pain to teach teens about the painful experiences of adulthood. What are some difficult challenges of adulthood?
   - What are the pros and cons of wilderness or adventure programs where harsh conditions and strict discipline are supposed to make teens grow-up?
   - Some people believe high school graduates should be forced to move away from parents and friends and work for at least a year before going to college or vocational school. Discuss the benefits and drawbacks.

The Journey to Maturity

Freeze Tag

1. Who or what is your IT? _____
2. How did IT tag you? _____
   _____

3. How have you been frozen regarding your thoughts? _____
   _____
   _____

4. How have you been frozen regarding your feelings? _____
   _____
   _____

5. How have you been frozen regarding your actions or inactions? _____
   _____
   _____

**Depict or describe yourself mobilizing to move forward;
show or tell where you'll be going and what you'll be doing:**

TEENS – It's Time to Grow Up

Freeze Tag

FOR THE FACILITATOR

I. **Purpose**

To recognize when frozen or stuck and to mobilize internal and external resources to become un-stuck.

II. **General Comments**

Teens compare the childhood game to standing still in life; they are encouraged to move forward.

III. **Possible Activities**

a. Before session ask a few teens to practice playing freeze tag by walking (not running) and standing in place when tagged by the player who is *IT*.

b. They demonstrate the game at the start of session and peers guess that they are playing freeze tag.

c. Ask teens whether it is possible to be frozen in a moment of time or a stage of life. Examples:
- Some never grow up, live with and are supported by parents well into adulthood.
- Some were told *You will never amount to anything*, and they stop trying.

d. Distribute the *Freeze Tag* handout and allow time for completion.

e. Encourage teens to share their responses. Possibilities:
1. *It* might be an abuser, a drug, a crisis, family break up or loss of a loved one.
2. *It* might tag you with self-blame, addiction, isolation, loneliness.
3. Thoughts might be frozen in put-downs, self-pity, re-living the event.
4. Feelings might be frozen in fear, guilt, anger, sadness, jealousy, inferiority.
5. Actions might be stuck in bullying, fighting, self-harm attempts, blaming. Inaction might be to wait for rescue (as in freeze tag), to avoid moving ahead, or to refuse help.

Ways to mobilize might include these actions:
- Recognize that you are *frozen* and decide to move.
- Realize no one will rescue you, but people will help you if you are receptive.
- If you think you failed, realize you learned what doesn't work; keep trying.

Thomas Edison said *"I never failed. I just learned 10,000 things that don't work."*
- For fear of the unknown, each day take baby steps out of your comfort zone.
- *Thaw* resentment through forgiveness.
- Use positive self-talk to overcome negative messages from childhood.
- Make a gratitude list to stop self-pity.
- People with addictions, stuck at an age or stage, can be freed.
- Children who were abused may not thrive; therapy helps them flourish.

IV. **Enrichment Activities**

a. Ask teens if positive experiences can *freeze* people. Possible responses: a high school football hero with a sports scholarship may fear he won't do as well in athletics and academics in college; a prom queen may think that no adult role will be as fulfilling; a skateboard champion wants to stay in the skate park; young people who win acting, art, singing or other awards may think they reached their peak.

b. Ask teens how people with early achievements might *un-freeze*. Possibilities: They might not always be the best, but they can always do their best; early recognition feels good, but facing challenges and change is worthy of self-praise; fulfillment is found in many ways.

c. Encourage a discussion regarding being a big fish in a little pond or the opposite. Possible concepts: the big fish in the little pond has no need or room to grow; the little fish in the big ocean has different fish to emulate, new and better shores, bigger waves.

The Journey to Maturity

GLADIATOR OR GOPHER?

1. Your family argues a lot.

2. A street fight starts and you hate violence.

3. Two of your best friends are complaining about a third friend who is not present.

4. You are being threatened and fear retaliation if you speak out.

5. You are being pressured to do something against your principles.

6. Your respected relative criticizes the way you look and dress.

7. A favorite family member harshly criticizes your weight.

8. Your coach criticized your performance by calling you names and hurling insults.

9. A teacher made a hurtful comment to you in front of classmates.

10. A caregiver puts down your career aspirations.

11. Your neighbors leave their dogs out in zero degree weather or intense heat.

12. Your older siblings brag frequently about being better at sports or scholastics.

13. You have mood swings, sadness and angry outbursts.

14. You crave alcohol, drugs or cigarettes.

15. You feel torn in too many directions by school, sports, work, friends and family.

16. You feel the world is passing you by.

17. You fear people will make fun of you because of your strong faith.

18. Your dating partner flirts with others in front of you and behind your back.

19. Your date is under the influence of a substance and insists on driving you home.

20. You like people who are your same sex or wish you were the opposite sex.

21. Your friends litter the parking lot with food wrappers.

22. You concern yourself about people who are homeless.

23. Your caregivers treat you like a young child and won't let you get a driver's permit.

24. A dating partner you really like makes racial and ethnic slurs.

TEENS – It's Time to Grow Up

GLADIATOR OR GOPHER?

FOR THE FACILITATOR

I. Purpose
   To adopt the positive aspects of the *gladiator mentality* and avoid dangerous extremes.

II. General Comments
   Teens usually relate to sports concepts and many like movies about gladiators; the analogies apply to adolescent and adult life. People need to confront issues head on (with common sense) rather than retreat.

III. Possible Activities
   a. If possible show a picture of a gladiator and a gopher, write on board *gladiator mentality*.
   b. Ask teens to define the term (to play a sport despite pain; ancient gladiators fought to their death).
   c. Ask teens to describe gophers (rodent that burrows beneath the ground; person who avoids issues).
   d. Encourage a discussion about sports stars who sustained injuries but kept on playing.
   e. Discuss pros (team heroes) and cons (injuries worsened and impairments affected their lives).
   f. Emphasize that a bold stance is enabling in adolescence and adulthood, to an extent.
   g. Give a volunteer host the *Gladiator or Gopher* handout. Host reads the statements.
      Teens take turns stating reactions of a foolish gladiator, an avoidant gopher, and a wise gladiator.
      Possible responses:
      There are no right or wrong answers; teens may ask peers for help.

Foolish Gladiator	Gopher	Wise Gladiator
1. Jump into the argument.	Ignore the issue.	Suggest counseling.
2. Yell from the sidewalk, Stop!	Never walk the street again.	Leave! Anonymously call police.
3. You and the friend fight them.	Ignore their comments.	Suggest they speak to the friend.
4. Threaten them back.	Say nothing to no one.	Tell a trusted adult.
5. Attack their lack of morals.	Don't commit to yes or no.	Simply say no.
6. Tell the person to back off.	Say nothing.	Say you prefer to be unique.
7. Say It's none of your business.	Be sad about your weight.	Consider if the comment is valid.
8. Yell back.	Sulk in sorrow.	Share feelings with coach alone.
9. Slam down your book.	Run out of the room.	Talk with teacher after class.
10. Tell caregiver to butt out.	Change your goals.	Pursue your passion.
11. Ring their bell and yell.	Stay out of their business.	Tell them your concerns.
12. Remind them of their faults.	Feel inferior.	Find and focus on your strengths.
13. Fight, put on a brave face.	Isolate so no one knows.	Ask for help at home or school.
14. Throw them down the toilet.	Struggle alone.	Get help from a trusted adult.
15. Keep doing it all.	Say you're sick and sleep.	Decide what goes and what stays.
16. Blame others for your misery.	Let life go on around you.	Do something for others.
17. Call them sinners and bigots.	Keep quiet about your beliefs.	Show faith by your actions.
18. Accuse and argue loudly.	Suffer in silence.	Discuss options with partner.
19. Grab the wheel.	Ride along and hope for safety.	Find a safe way home.
20. Argue and shout about rights.	Hide in the closet.	Be true to your identity.
21. Insist they pick up their mess.	Leave the mess.	Ask them to help you clean up.
22. Criticize heartless people.	Care but do nothing.	Volunteer at a shelter or program.
23. Shout that you're grown-up.	Give up.	Prove maturity; act responsibly.
24. Call him/her a prejudiced pig.	Keep quiet to keep peace.	Share your concerns.

IV. Enrichment Activities
   Ask teens to share their personal funniest, most embarrassing or most amazing gladiator and gopher moments.

Am I There Yet?

1. I think I'm invincible; it won't happen to me.
2. My actions are my business; they shouldn't bother anyone else.
3. I consider options and weigh pros and cons.
4. I say *No* to myself when tempted to do wrong.
5. I tend to be impatient and demanding.
6. I repeat many of the same mistakes.
7. I am dependable, have good attendance and punctuality.
8. I'm a victim; it is never my fault.
9. I'm in control of my actions and reactions.
10. I often play when it is time to work.
11. I feel entitled to privileges without learning them.
12. I have a right to my own opinions.
13. I expect life to be fair.
14. I treat others as I want to be treated.
15. I have trouble making and acting on decisions.
16. I prefer my own way and rarely compromise.
17. I usually give in to peer pressure.
18. I believe all people have value.
19. I need no one but myself.
20. Reaching the top is important, not how I get there.
21. I dwell on the negative things that happened to me.
22. I choose positive role models.
23. I try to be the center of attention.
24. I don't need or take advice.
25. I am often a doormat.
26. I speak, e-mail or text first and think later.
27. My actions back up my words.
28. I have the right to retaliate or get even.

TEENS – It's Time to Grow Up

Am I There Yet?

FOR THE FACILITATOR

I. Purpose
To recognize signs of immaturity and maturity.

II. General Comments
Teens develop insight into responsible and healthy adult thoughts and actions.

III. Possible Activities
a. Before session label one large piece of paper *Agree* and another *Disagree*; post on opposite walls.
b. Cut the *Are Am I There Yet?* handout on the broken lines; place slips face down in a container.
c. If possible arrange chairs along walls, or pull chairs away to allow standing room under the signs.
d. Ask teens in what context they have heard or said *Are we there yet?* (road trips).
e. Explain that *Am I There Yet?* requires honesty to determine how close they are to adulthood.
f. Teens take turns pulling a slip from the container and reading it aloud.
g. Peers move to the *Agree* or *Disagree* wall based on their true beliefs and actions.
h. The teen who pulled the slip calls on peers to substantiate their responses and give examples.

Concepts to elicit
1. Immature teens think they are invincible; they engage in reckless behavior with little fear of harm.
2. Immature teens do not realize how their behavior impacts others positively or negatively.
3. Mature teens use intelligent problem solving skills.
4. Mature teens can restrict their own impulses and consider consequences.
5. Immature teens expect to get what they want when they want it or they whine or complain.
6. Immature teens do not learn from mistakes.
7. Mature teens show up as scheduled and on time; they show self-discipline.
8. Immature teens play a helpless role and blame others.
9. Mature teens realize they cannot control people or events but can decide how to respond.
10. Immature teens prefer short term pleasure rather than long-term rewards for diligence.
11. Immature teens have a sense of entitlement and expect goodies to be handed to them.
12. Mature teens assertively but respectfully express their beliefs.
13. Immature teens are easily upset by unfairness; they do not accept that injustice occurs.
14. Mature teens can put themselves in other people's shoes and follow the Golden Rule.
15. Immature teens lack confidence to choose and follow a path.
16. Immature teens do not recognize the benefits of give and take or win-win outcomes.
17. Immature teens tend to follow the crowd, usually to fit in or because they fear rejection.
18. Mature teens recognize everyone's worth, even those who are different or devalued by society.
19. Immature teens fail to appreciate interdependence among people working toward common goals.
20. Immature teens want to win regardless of whom they hurt or trample.
21. Immature teens give-in to self-pity rather than seek help to force themselves forward.
22. Mature teens choose role models who use their abilities to better the world.
23. Immature teens want the spotlight (for negative or positive behavior); they won't share the glory.
24. Immature teens refuse to listen to and evaluate potential wise counsel.
25. Immature teens let others walk all over them; they may allow abuse or allow themselves to be used by others.
26. Immature teens communicate impulsively; they don't think about harm until it's too late.
27. Mature teens behave in alignment with their spoken beliefs and intentions.
28. Immature teens don't know that two wrongs don't make a right and stoop to their offender's level.

IV. Enrichment Activities
- Provide copies of the uncut handout.
- Make a roadmap for students with 28 squares on the road. Have them color or fill in the squares as it refers to where they are, to see visually how well they are in their planning and "adulthood".

Perspectives (It's All How You Look at It)

The moment one gives close attention to anything, even a blade of grass, it becomes a mysterious, awesome, indescribably magnificent world in itself. ~ Henry Miller

Who or what is a person, place, thing, or idea of yours that has always been a part of your life?
___

From your perspective when you were a child, describe the above ___
___

From your perspective now, as teen, describe the above ___
___

When you become an adult, how do you think your perspective will change on the above? ___
___

TEENS – It's Time to Grow Up

Perspectives (It's All How You Look at It)

FOR THE FACILITATOR

I. Purpose
To identify that age and perspective affect experiences and emotions.

II. General Comments
Teens look back, within and forward prompted by people, places, things and ideas.

III. Possible Activities
a. Display an object like a pen and ask teens what it means to them (writing tool).

b. Ask how it might seem different to a child, teen and adult (child – for scribbling; teen – for homework; adult – to write checks).

c. Ask teens for examples of objects seen differently through child, teen and adult eyes. Possibility:

A flower to a child looks and smells beautiful, it's a treasure to give to mom; to a teen it's the prom or the fragrance of first love; to an adult it's a wedding bouquet or a funeral wreath.

d. Distribute the *Perspectives (It's All How You Look at It)* handout; encourage teens to write a few sentences or paragraph about a person, place, thing or idea as perceived during each stage.

e. Encourage teens to use as many of the senses as possible and to describe their feelings.

f. Encourage teens to share their work. Examples:

Person – A parent to the child may be seen as larger than life, loving or brutal, a soothing or booming voice, a gentle or harsh touch; to the teen a parent may be a confidant or a disciplinarian or unreasonable; to the adult, a parent may be a source of strength or a burden or the voice of reason.

Place – Home to the child may be a safe haven or a place with scary sights and sounds like angry faces and shouting; to a grounded teen, home is a prison; to the adult, it's a dream house, a mortgage, a hellhole, a status symbol.

Thing – A car to the child means a ride to the park; to the teen it's liberty, responsibility, dating; the engine's hum is music to the ears; to the adult, it's another bill, a necessity; gas fumes are annoying reminders of soaring prices.

Idea – Honesty to the child may be finding a dollar on the candy store floor and turning it in; to the teen who ditched school it's telling the truth to caregivers; to the adult, truth might be admitting mistakes to one's children.

IV. Enrichment Activities
a. Write the quote on the board ***Be careful how you interpret the world: It is like that.*** ~ Erich Heller

b. Ask teens to analyze its meaning (how we see and think about things become our reality).

c. Ask teens how the same situation might be interpreted differently and its effects. Examples:

Event	Negative interpretation	Positive Interpretation
A peer doesn't say *Hello*.	The person's mad at me; I feel angry or rejected.	The person is probably deep in thought; I get it.
I receive a failing grade.	I can't learn anything; I feel hopeless.	I need better study habits and peer tutoring; I feel encouraged.
Someone else won a contest or was picked for the team.	I'm a loser; I'll stop trying; I feel inadequate.	I had fun trying. I'll work harder or try a different challenge; I feel empowered.

Continuums

Inflexible _____ Adaptable	Uninspired _____ Enthusiastic
Give up _____ Stick to it	Put self down _____ Celebrate small victories
Lose Time _____ Manage time	Must win _____ Win-win
Dissatisfied _____ Thankful	Focus on pain _____ Focus on gain
Selfish _____ Selfless	I can't _____ How can I?
Crunch myself _____ Stretch myself	Hoarder _____ Giver
Stuck _____ Move forward	Beat myself up _____ Learn from mistakes
Procrastinate _____ Do it now	Suspicious _____ Trustful
Directed by others _____ Self-directed	Resentful _____ Forgiving
Blame _____ Take responsibility	Low self-esteem _____ Confident
No self-control _____ Self-disciplined	Dishonest _____ Honest
Impulsive _____ Deliberate	Drifter _____ Goal-oriented
Unreliable _____ Able to be counted on	See the glass half empty _____ Half full

Select five traits most meaningful to you. Write their labels on the lines above the continuums. Place an "x" on your location. *Example*:

Aloof   *Friendly*

_____ x _____

The person in the above example might be considered a loner, except for a few close friends.

TEENS – It's Time to Grow Up

Continuums

FOR THE FACILITATOR

I. **Purpose**
   To acquire self-knowledge about traits and values; to look at extremes and middle of the road options.

II. **General Comments**
   Teens identify where they are, where they want to be, and how to get there.

III. **Possible Activities**
   a. Copy the following on the board:
      Cold _____Hot
   b. Ask a volunteer to mark lukewarm with an "x" on the scale (teen will place it about midpoint).
   c. Put another continuum on the board with labels: *People pleaser* and *Please myself.*
   d. Encourage a discussion about the two extremes (one bends over backward and is a doormat; the other is self-absorbed and considers no one else's needs or feelings).
   e. Explain that on some scales teens might be at an extreme; on others, more toward the middle.
   f. Distribute the *Continuums* handout; ask a couple of volunteers to read aloud the scales.
   g. Urge teens to thoughtfully select the scales where they would like their "x" to be more to the right (to approve of themselves).
   h. Emphasize there are no right or wrong locations; teens show what is true for them.
   i. Allow time for completion.
   j. Encourage teens to put their most meaningful scales on the board and show their locations.
   k. Teens state where they wish to be, and why.
   l. Teens receive peer feedback on ways to reach the spot that they identified as ideal for themselves.

IV. **Enrichment Activities**
   a. Encourage teens to give and substantiate their opinions: Possible thoughts are parenthesized.
      - Is it possible to be too intentional or goal-oriented? (Yes; might miss out on unplanned opportunities or spontaneous fun).
      - What does it mean to stretch yourself? (To seek challenges and grow, even if not the winner or the best).
      - Give an example of being too honest (To give unsolicited, untactful feedback).
      - What is healthy selfishness? (To take care of self to be able to help others).
      - Can a person be too trusting? (Yes, with unknown people where safety is at risk).
      - Give an example of celebrating small victories (Pat self on the back for positive self-talk).
   b. Ask teens to brainstorm other scales as a volunteer lists them on the board.
   c. Teens rate themselves on the scales and discuss how they might move toward their goal spots.

The Journey to Maturity

Sex Sense

**As you mature, your sexual self emerges.
React to the questions most important to you. You do not need to share your responses.**

- Describe your opinion about sexually explicit movies and their effect on teens.
- Describe your opinion about sexually explicit music videos and their effect on teens.
- Describe your opinion about sexually explicit Internet sites and their effect on teens.
- Describe your opinion about sexually explicit television shows and their effect on teens.
- Describe your opinion about sexually explicit song lyrics and their effect on teens.
- Is it possible to keep a boyfriend or girlfriend without having sex? Explain.
- Do you believe that *everyone is doing it?* Explain your reasons.
- Does safe sex exist? Explain your reasons.
- What are your thoughts about sexual abstinence?
- What do you know about sexually transmitted diseases (STD) and where to obtain information and medical recommendations?
- What life-altering decisions would one have to make if that person became pregnant?
- What life-altering decisions would one have to make if that person's sexual partner became pregnant?
- Do you think pornography addiction is similar to drug addiction? Explain your reasons.
- What are some challenges faced by people who experience same sex attraction?
- What challenges might a person have who is considering a sex change operation?
- How might a person who was raped obtain help?
- How might a person who was sexually or physically abused obtain help?
- Do you believe emotional abuse by a partner can be as damaging as physical violence? Explain.
- What are your thoughts about teens in abusive relationships who to stay with abusive partners?
- What is your solution to which bathrooms cross-dressers use.
- In what ways does faith affect sexuality?
- In what ways do values affect sexuality?
- How do you respond if someone says, *"If you love me, you will ..."*
- Does it matter how long you date or know someone before having sex? Explain.
- Before dating someone, how important is it to find out if the other person has had other sexual relations and if they could have a disease? Explain.
- In what ways other than sex can one show affection for a partner?
- Do you think that friends think teens are cool if they have sex? Explain.
- How does peer pressure play a part in teens having sex?
- What are your thoughts about having sex without caring about the person (friends with benefits)?
- What are your opinions on abortion, a teen having and raising a baby, or giving the baby up for adoption?
- How does one say *No?*
- In your opinion, what constitutes *having sex*?
- What are your thoughts about masturbation?
- What are your thoughts about pornography?
- What are your thoughts about saving sex for a marriage or a committed relationship as an adult?

TEENS – It's Time to Grow Up

Sex Sense

FOR THE FACILITATOR

I. **Purpose**

To consider how sexual decisions affect life.

To ask thought-provoking questions; not to advise or judge.

II. **General Comments**

Teens are bombarded by societal sexuality and are affected by puberty's hormonal changes. Most are aware about types of sex – oral, anal and vaginal. Some teens engage in phone sex and cyber sex; spreading explicit information and photos via texts and social media have led to humiliation and suicides.

III. **Possible Activities**

a. Write *Sex Sense* on the board; ask teens what it means (to use intelligence and judgment regarding sex).

b. Ask teens what sexual issues people face (accept any responses).

c. Explain that they will have the chance to think about sex-related issues that may affect their lives.

d. Distribute the *Sex Sense* handout and ask teens to read the page silently.

e. Ask teens to respond in writing to at least three questions; reinforce that their responses are private.

f. Allow time for completion.

g. Depending on the group's maturity and comfort level, allow teens to share responses if they wish.

h. Most questions have no right or wrong answers but for issues related to sexually transmitted diseases, contraception, pregnancy, physical and emotional abuse and rape, teens are assisted by their primary care physicians, local medical and mental health departments, rape crisis centers, family planning clinics, free HIV testing programs, etc.

i. Encourage teens to talk to their parents about sexual issues if possible.

j. Encourage teens to meet with the school nurse and counselor as needed.

k. Encourage teens to consult medical and mental health professionals about gender change options or other concerns.

l. Follow obligatory reporting requirements regarding physical, psychological, emotional and sexual abuse.

m. Some concepts to elicit regarding the questions:

- ***Do you believe that everybody is doing it?*** No, despite media messages, many teens remain virgins.
- ***Does safe sex exist?*** Probably not; to abstain is the best and only perfect birth control and disease prevention technique. Emotionally, safe sex is difficult to achieve because one may take it very seriously and the other may view it as a casual, impulsive encounter.
- ***In your opinion, what constitutes having sex?*** Some teens engage in mutual masturbation, phone or cyber-sex or think anything except vaginal sex is not sex. Emotional, social and physical issues result from these other forms of intimacy: possible extreme attachment (maybe one-sided); secret acts emerging via gossip or electronic communication; diseases transmitted from any blood or body fluid contact.

IV. **Enrichment Activities**

Encourage teens in teams or individually to research online information regarding topics of interest to them. National and local governmental public health websites provide data and resources.

LIFE AFTER HIGH SCHOOL 7

If you don't take charge of shaping your own destiny, others will apply their agenda to you.
— Eric Allenbaugh

Future Feud .... page 105 ▶

In a Family Feud-type game, teens brainstorm about probable and questionable places to meet a dating partner; things within and outside oneself to consider when choosing a career; what to consider when choosing a school or training program. Teens are encouraged to compose other questions and brainstorm, discuss and debate topics they see as important.

Your Vision .... page 107 ▶

Teens see with the mind's eye, depict, describe and believe. Teens personalize famous quotes about a beginning, castles in the air and a different drummer. Teens are encouraged to use non-verbal expression – to draw, use symbols or cartoons and/or verbal elaboration.

Do What You Love .... page 109 ▶

Teens compare the ways dogs enjoy life and fulfill their roles to their own future and identify ways they will enjoy simple things, dig deep within, chase a dream. They consider the hoops they might jump through and their rewards. Teens think about work for money versus work for the love of it and note career ladder opportunities.

Love .... page 111 ▶

Through Shakespeare's Sonnet 116 teens ponder the kind of love they may want in the future; teens interpret aspects of grown-up committed love then brainstorm traits to look for in a dating partner.

Life after High School

Future Feud

Name ten possible places to meet a dating partner:
1. House of worship or spiritual group
2. School
3. Work or volunteer job
4. Humanitarian organization, fundraiser for a cause you believe in, political rally
5. Museum, art gallery, library
6. Pet show, dog park or animal shelter
7. Sports team or events, skate park, well-attended beach, coffee shop on a busy corner
8. Music, art, dance or other class
9. Store related to your interests like a book, sporting goods or music store
10. Concert, community theater, conference, writing, painting or other club

Name ten things within yourself to consider when choosing a career:
1. Your interests
2. Your physical abilities
3. Your common sense, intellectual abilities, skills learned at home and self-taught skills
4. Your people skills
5. Your level of stress tolerance
6. Your preference for a day job or willingness to work evenings and week-ends
7. Your preference to work close to home or travel
8. Your level of tolerance for highs, lows, and rejection as in sales occupations and show business
9. Your preference to lead, manage, or to keep a lower profile
10. Your preference for working with information systems or with your hands

Name five things outside yourself to consider when choosing an occupation:
1. Labor market – is there a need for your product or service?
2. Geography – Where will you find the job? (If you plan to open a surf shop you need to be near an ocean).
3. Finances – What is the cost to start a business? The job's earning potential?
4. Workplace environment – Casual or formal? Routine and regimented or less predictable and creative?
5. Level of supervision – Lots of guidance? More personal freedom? Level of responsibility?

Name five things to consider when choosing a school or training program:
1. Cost, availability of grants or scholarships, student loans; years of debt
2. The school's reputation for excellence and job placement
3. Availability of work-study programs on campus or part-time work nearby
4. Comparison of costs and grants and loans: adult education, community colleges, private and state universities.
5. Proximity to home or necessity for dorm or off-campus housing

TEENS – It's Time to Grow Up

Future Feud

FOR THE FACILITATOR

I. Purpose
To consider relationship, career and school issues in young adulthood.

II. General Comments
Teens play a Family Feud-type game and brainstorm about decisions they will face.

III. Possible Activities
a. Ask teens to describe how Family Feud games are played (families compete to name the most popular survey responses).
b. Explain that teens will play a version in which two teams or *families* will brainstorm responses.
c. Distribute the *Future Feud* handout to the game show host who will read survey questions aloud.
d. A scorekeeper tracks responses for each team; one point per response.
e. A timekeeper makes teams stop after one minute.
f. Divide teens into two teams; teammates sit together on opposite sides of the room.
g. The host reads the first survey question; teams take one minute turns responding.
h. One team may name all the responses or after one minute the opposing team adds to the list.
i. When the specified number of responses is given, the host asks the next question.
j. Any reasonable or substantiated responses are acceptable.
k. The handout provides possible responses for only host and facilitator to see; host may reveal them if all contestants are stumped.
l. The team with the most points wins.
m. Ask teens to brainstorm other survey questions relevant to adulthood and to play the game as above. Possibilities:
   - Questionable places to meet a dating partner.
   - Things to consider when buying a car or house.
   - Things to consider before becoming a partnership.
   - Things to consider when planning the number of children to have.

IV. Enrichment Activities
Encourage teens to discuss and debate related issues. Possibilities:
- Which is more important and why: high salary or job satisfaction?
- Is it a good idea for spouses or family members work closely together? Explain.
- Which is more important: quality or quantity of work and why?
- What are the advantages and disadvantages of labor unions?
- Is it advisable to date a co-worker? Explain.
- What is an example of a career ladder? Give an example.
- Are there dead-end jobs? Substantiate your opinion.

Your Vision

Imagine and then draw, doodle, sketch cartoons or use symbols in a collage format in the boxes below, to personalize one or more of the following quotes.

Use the back of this page or a separate piece of paper to elaborate.

There will be a time when you believe everything is finished. That will be the beginning.
~ Louis L'Amour

If you have built castles in the air, your work need not be lost; that is where they should be. Now put the foundations under them.
~ Henry David Thoreau

If a man does not keep pace with his companions, perhaps it is because he hears a different drummer. Let him step to the music which he hears, however measured or far away.
~ Henry David Thoreau

TEENS – It's Time to Grow Up

Your Vision

FOR THE FACILITATOR

I. **Purpose**
   To use non-verbal expression regarding a beginning, dreams and goals, and individualization.

II. **General Comments**
   Teens are encouraged to first imagine and then depict, describe, and believe.

III. **Possible Activities**
   a. If possible provide large paper, pencils, crayons, colored markers and/or paint.
   b. Ask teens to discuss their views about the saying *A picture is worth a thousand words*.
   c. Explain that drawing, even using stick figures or symbols, helps to become in touch with daydreams and feelings.
   d. Stress that artistic ability is irrelevant; they will have a vision and put it on paper; they will choose whether to share their pictures.
   e. Encourage teens to work quietly to allow peers to get into their own heads and hearts.
   f. Distribute the *Your Vision* handout and let teens choose which quote to draw, or cut photocopies between the boxes and distribute one of the three choices to each teen.
   g. Allow time for completion of drawings.
   h. Teens may title their visions and draw or write their thoughts in the quotation boxes.
   i. Encourage teens to show their pictures if they wish and/or to share their visions and thoughts verbally. Possibilities:
      - Teens may believe everything is finished at graduation; yet it begins the rest of their lives. They may envision college, career, marriage, children, and specific achievements.
      - Teens may believe everything is finished after a break up; yet there will be other loves in life to look forward to.
      - Teens need to build castles in the air, to have high hopes; then to make them happen with a plan and hard work.
      - Teens need to listen and march to their unique drummer, their calling; they need to sharpen their skills and hear people who say their aspirations are not realistic but then decide for themselves.

IV. **Enrichment Activities**
   a. Ask teens to share one insight that emerged by drawing that words might not have revealed.
   b. Encourage a discussion about other forms of non-verbal expression (sculpt, design collages with magazine cut-outs; take up photography; create scrap books; discover crafts, music, dance, sports; design and nurture a garden; collect objects of nature).
   c. Encourage teens to recall quotes they have read or heard or to compose their own words of wisdom and then depict them.
   d. Ask teens to compose a 6-words-bit-of-wisdom quotation of their own.
      Example: *Stand up for what you believe.*

Life after High School

Do What You Love

If you have seen a dog …
- Snooze in the sun
- Eat with gusto
- Hide a treat
- Dig for treasure
- Chase a ball
- Catch a Frisbee
- Swim or surf
- Jump over hurdles
- Lick a face
- Listen
- Love
- Serve as eyes, ears, hands and feet
- Protect
- Rescue
- Herd or pull a sled (fulfill an inborn role)

Then you know that dogs do what they love and love what they do.

I will enjoy simple things like _____

_____

_____

I will dig deep to uncover this within me _____

_____

_____

I will chase my dream with all my heart by _____

_____

_____

I will jump through these hoops _____

_____

_____

My rewards will be _____

_____

_____

TEENS – It's Time to Grow Up

Do What You Love
FOR THE FACILITATOR

I. **Purpose**
   To live with enthusiasm, dream big and pursue one's passion.

II. **General Comments**
   Teens consider how dogs enjoy life and do what they were born to do wholeheartedly.

III. **Possible Activities –**
   a. Write on the board *Dog and Pony Show* and ask its meaning (elaborate presentation to promote a product or impress).
   b. Encourage a discussion of dog shows and championship requirements (face and form, obedience).
   c. Ask teens: If you were a dog, would you want to prance around a ring, diet strictly and be groomed incessantly to make yourself or your handler look good? (probably not).
   d. Ask teens to compare a show dog's life to a pet dog (who gets dirty, plays and lounges freely).
   e. Ask about other roles dogs play (law enforcement, serve people with disabilities, search and rescue, emotional therapy. Their work might be to sniff for bombs or herd sheep. Dogs also compete in agility trials where ability, not appearance wins the prize.)
   f. Ask in what ways teens might be in a *Dog and Pony Show* (try to impress peers by appearance or clothes, compete for grades or act cool to be accepted; pursue a career to please a parent).
   g. Distribute the *Do What You Love* handout; volunteers read aloud *If you have seen a dog...* list.
   h. Allow time for completion.
   i. Encourage teens to share their responses. Possibilities:
      - *Enjoy simple things like...* a walk in the woods, solitude, a ride on a skateboard, etc.
      - *Dig deep to uncover this within me ...* compassion, talent, my voice, my purpose, etc.
      - *Chase my dream with all my heart by ...* further study to develop my gifts, etc.
      - *Jump through these hoops ...* refute negative comments; try again after set-backs, etc.
      - *Rewards will be ...* to fulfill my chosen role, to be the real deal and my best self, etc.

IV. **Enrichment Activities**
   a. Ask teens to consider a mother dog and her pups and brainstorm her nurturing behavior:
      - Feed, warm and protect the pups; discipline, encourage exploration and nudge toward independence.
   b. Ask teens how they might pursue their passion in similar ways:
      - *Feed* it with positive thoughts, information and education.
      - *Keep it warm and alive* as they tell others, write about and draw their intended achievement.
      - *Discipline* themselves to practice the skill, study or volunteer in related endeavors.
      - *Explore* all possible ways to do what they love as a hobby or their life's work.
      - *Nudge* themselves to make time, earn money, find the energy and seek mentors, etc.
   c. Write on the board the Henry David Thoreau quote:
      Do not hire a man who does your work for money, but him who does it for the love of it.
      Ask teens what they think about this bit of wisdom and why.
   d. Ask teens how they might do what they love on a career ladder. Examples:
      - You want to become a doctor but medical training is too lengthy or costly – become a physician assistant, a nurse or nurse practitioner, an occupational, physical or speech therapist, a sports physical therapist or a mental health therapist.
      - You hope to become a TV comedian – do local comedy nights until discovered.
      - You didn't make the major leagues –teach physical education and coach high school teams.
      - You don't have years or finances right now to spend in law school; become a paralegal.

Life after High School

Love
Sonnet 116

Let me not to the marriage of true minds
Admit impediments. Love is not love
Which alters when it alteration finds,
Or bends with the remover to remove:
O, no! it is an ever fixed mark,
That looks on tempests and is never shaken;
It is the star to every wandering bark,
Whose worth's unknown, although its height be taken.
Love's not Time's fool, though rosy lips and cheeks
Within his bending sickle's compass come:
Love alters not with his brief hours and weeks,
But bears it out even to the edge of doom.
If this be error and upon me proved,
I never writ nor no man ever loved.

~ William Shakespeare

What is the most surprising word in this poem? Why?

Love

FOR THE FACILITATOR

I. **Purpose**
   To consider grown-up committed love.

II. **General Comments**
   Teens are encouraged to ponder the kind of love they may want in their future.

III. **Possible Activities**
   a. Write *Love* on the board and ask teens what it means to them; accept any responses.
   b. Explain that they will read a sonnet about love.
   c. Explain that good literature is open to a variety of interpretations; it has different meanings depending on the reader's point of view.
   d. Distribute the *Love* handout; two volunteers to take turns reading the poem aloud as peers read silently.
   e. Encourage teens to highlight phrases that are meaningful to them or that they wonder about.
   f. Before teens write, remind them there no right or wrong responses.
   g. Allow time to complete the handout.
   h. Encourage teens to share their thoughts and feelings about the poem.
   i. Encourage teens to share their most surprising word and why.
   j. Ask teens to apply their impressions of the poem to the type of relationship they have or hope to have in the future.

IV. **Enrichment Activities**
   a. Ask the following questions; accept any interpretations. Possibilities are parenthesized.
      - What might *marriage* mean in the poem? (unity between like-minded people).
      - What is an impediment? (a hurdle or obstacle).
      - What is said about love and change? (love remains faithful).
      - How does love weather storms? (it remains unshaken).
      - What does *the star to every wandering bark* mean? (the North Star giving direction to a lost ship).
      - Explain that *Whose worth's unknown, although its height be taken* may mean the star's value is unknown although its elevation above the horizon can be measured.
      - Ask *How does this relate to love?* (love's depth and power are not fully understood).
      - What is said about love and time? (love continues despite declines in appearance or other damages).
      - How long does love endure? (to death or through eternity).
   b. Ask teens in teams or as a group to brainstorm positive traits to look for in a mate. Possibilities:
      - Shows responsibility at work and school; drives safely.
      - Communicates openly; does not try to manipulate or confuse partner.
      - Shares similar values and lifestyle; is honest and ethical.
      - Shows respect to parents, partner, friends, self.
      - Does not stoop to jealous behaviors and does not try to make partner suspicious.
      - Displays self-motivation and encourages partner to pursue independent interests.
      - Maintains a positive outlook; sees humor but understands heartbreak.
      - Works hard but seeks balance; has compatible goals regarding family, children, etc.
      - Knows the value of silence as well as the 'right' words.
      - Knows the importance of holding hands.

Whole Person Associates is the leading publisher of training resources for professionals who empower people to create and maintain healthy lifestyles. Our creative resources will help you work effectively with your clients in the areas of stress management, wellness promotion, mental health and life skills.

Please visit us at our web site: **www.wholeperson.com**. You can check out our entire line of products, place an order, request our print catalog, and sign up for our monthly special notifications.

Whole Person Associates

800-247-6789